I0644687

The DEI Practitioner's Handbook

The work of advancing and embedding diversity, equity, and inclusion (DEI) efforts within school systems requires a roadmap for success. This book provides step-by-step advice for any educator who is serving in the capacity of a DEI-related role, from a teacher or director to an assistant superintendent.

Author Erica Buchanan-Rivera takes you through the complexities and controversies of the work, the commonly shared roles and responsibilities of DEI practitioners, and pitfalls to avoid. She shows you how to create an inclusive institutional culture, which involves the work of building capacity and a common language for DEI, normalizing critical conversations, creating coalitions, and honoring human and civil rights. In addition, she helps you tackle challenging aspects of DEI roles such as dealing with resistance and pushback, responding to political and oppositional movements, plugging families into systems work, and protecting your wellness and peace.

Through detailed accounts that uplift experiences of DEI practitioners across the country, this powerful resource will help you understand how to thrive and navigate your crucial school and community role.

Erica Buchanan-Rivera is an educational equity scholar, consultant, community organizer, and fierce advocate for children and liberatory spaces where people can be their authentic selves. She has served as a teacher, principal, director of curriculum, and a district DEI administrator (e.g., Chief Equity Officer and Director of Equity and Inclusion) in a suburban and an urban school district. Buchanan-Rivera is an Assistant Professor in the Leadership, Language, and Curriculum Department of DePaul University, who brings a lens of justice into her educational leadership courses. She is also the author of the book, *Identity-Affirming Classrooms: Spaces that Center Humanity* (2022).

Equity and Social Justice in Education Series

Paul C. Gorski, Series Editor

Routledge's Equity and Social Justice in Education series is a publishing home for books that apply critical and transformative equity and social justice theories to the work of on-the-ground educators. Books in the series describe meaningful solutions to the racism, white supremacy, economic injustice, sexism, heterosexism, transphobia, ableism, neoliberalism, and other oppressive conditions that pervade schools and school districts.

Latina Pedagogies of Care
How Cariño Can Give Tired Teachers Power and Hope
Ale Babino and Rocío Almanza

Abolition in School Counseling
Practicing Liberation and Community in PK-12 Schools
Riley Drake and Alicia Oglesby

Navigating Power, Harnessing Possibility
A Guide for Leading Schools Through Uncertain Times
Mary Rice-Boothe

Community, Love, and Connection in Early Care and Education
An Interactive Guide for Holistic, Equitable Early Learning
Meghan L. Green, Lilly Padia, and Mariana Souto-Manning

Transformative Mindfulness in Education
Caring for Ourselves While Kindling Change
Rhiannon Kim

Teaching Indigenous Studies
An Introduction for K-12 Educators
Leilani Sabzalian, Meredith McCoy, and Helen Thomas

Peacebuilding Pedagogies
Racial Justice, Dialogue, and Belonging in the Classroom
Crystena Parker-Shandal

Cultivating Critical Advocacy
A Framework for Educators of Multilingual Learners
Rebecca E. Linares and Kate Seltzer

The DEI Practitioner's Handbook
A Guide for School and District Leaders in Pursuit of Educational Justice
Erica Buchanan-Rivera

The DEI Practitioner's Handbook

A Guide for School and District Leaders in Pursuit of Educational Justice

Erica Buchanan-Rivera

Routledge
Taylor & Francis Group
NEW YORK AND LONDON

Designed cover image: Getty Images and Shutterstock

First published 2027
by Routledge
605 Third Avenue, New York, NY 10158

and by Routledge
4 Park Square, Milton Park, Abingdon, Oxon, OX14 4RN

Routledge is an imprint of the Taylor & Francis Group, an informa business

ISBN: 978-1-032-60938-6 (pbk)
ISBN: 978-1-032-62354-2 (ebk)

DOI: 10.4324/9781032623542

Typeset in Palatino
by KnowledgeWorks Global Ltd.

Dedication

This is dedicated to the real ones. You know who you are. Keep showing up for children.

Contents

Figures

Foreword

There are moments in educational history when a book is more than timely; it is necessary. This work by Dr. Erica Buchanan-Rivera arrives at such a moment. In an era when the language of diversity, equity, and inclusion is questioned, politicized, and in some spaces erased, inequity in schools continues to operate with measurable consistency and long-term impact. Students still encounter barriers not because of their ability, but because our systems were never designed for them. This reality underscores the importance and urgency of the text you are holding.

With the current climate surrounding DEI roles and expectations, this book provides guidance and affirmation. Equity is not fading from schools; it is evolving. These pages remind us that core principles are not disappearing. They continue to shape decisions, culture, and human interactions even in the face of political resistance. The need for skilled, principled, research-driven DEI practitioners has never been greater. Dr. Buchanan-Rivera illuminates a path forward for those who embrace the moral imperative to build a just educational system.

For anyone stepping into DEI leadership, this book reinforces that progress is possible when courage and truth align with strategy. Dr. Buchanan-Rivera writes from inside the work, translating complex challenges into accessible, actionable understanding. She names the tensions, triumphs, and truths of equity implementation, and reminds us that leadership requires knowing when to push, when to pause, and when to protect our peace.

DEI practitioners navigate emotionally demanding terrain. The work calls for courage to confront misinformation, patience to pace initiatives wisely, and wisdom to discern when silence protects peace and when silence becomes complicity. This book reveals both the promise and the pitfalls of equity efforts. Its exploration of capacity building, organizational culture, legal responsibility, leadership development, and personal wellness makes it more than a guidebook. It is testimony. It is direction. It is affirmation that despite the noise, the backlash, and the fatigue, those doing the work remain present. The work continues.

Dwayne Chism, Ed.D.
Author of *Leading Your School Toward Equity*

A Note to the Reader

When I started writing this book, there was a high demand for roles aimed at improving and coordinating diversity, equity, and inclusion (DEI) efforts. I was my county's first Chief Equity and Inclusion Officer within a public school district. In subsequent years, neighboring districts began recruiting and hiring DEI roles. I often found myself mentoring other DEI practitioners and providing advice, while yearning for my own guidebook. My work was rooted in culturally responsive leadership, ancestral wisdom, collectivism, and often my own intuition. I used the power of my imagination to develop structures for professional learning, inclusive practices, and student advocacy, co-developing the first Central Indiana Black Student Leadership Summit under my leadership. I also strengthened my identity as a leader through hardships and political violence, learning how to use my voice and how to respond in the face of opposition. To heal and maintain my stamina in justice-centered work, I sought and built a community around me that reflected people across states who carried similar titles, responsibilities, and roles. I learned that I was not alone and felt validation from shared experiences.

Following political rhetoric pertaining to Critical Race Theory (CRT), I noticed an immediate shift in the pacing and visibility of DEI work. Many of my colleagues were informed to cease discussions about racial inequities with the rise of anti-CRT bills. The efforts of DEI practitioners in conservative counties were under scrutiny and often attacked. By this time, I was in my second DEI role and felt fortunate to work in a district where there was strong community support for responsive, inclusive, and affirming school environments. I was disheartened by the threats and negative publicity many colleagues were receiving with limited support from their institutions. I relived the trauma of my first DEI role through their experiences and, in some cases, resignations.

When the anti-DEI movement emerged, I was not surprised to see many school districts abandon their commitments of advancing equity. It was easy for leaders to abandon practices or positions they never authentically supported. The addition of anti-DEI executive orders became a convenient excuse for many educational leaders to dismantle DEI-related departments, roles, initiatives, and student activities without considering strategies for sustainability. School districts, one by one, were exposed for performative actions and confirmed the political nature of education.

While writing this book in an anti-DEI era, I was concerned that my work would not find an audience. Educators were advised to take down inclusive posters, schools discontinued affinity spaces, and numerous diversity, equity, and inclusion professionals were asked to adopt new titles instead of being identified as DEI practitioners. Internally, I struggled with the idea of publishing a book that discussed the roles and responsibilities of positions that were literally unraveling before my eyes. I also worried about the reactions of people who would view the title of my book and question, *Why is she publishing a DEI book? Doesn't she know that DEI is dead and we are being forced to focus on 'merit' now?*

As I wrestled with these reflections, I continued to support schools, students, and myself through consulting and professional learning experiences. While being in community with others and engaging in conversations, I have learned that DEI continues to live despite government overreach and executive orders. I consistently observe administrators and educators engaging in conversations about educational equity and approaches to remove institutional barriers. I have participated in conferences where most sessions covered equity concepts or addressed issues related to racial justice. I have talked to DEI practitioners who may have experienced a title change, yet continue to foster collective work in efforts to address inequities and accessibility concerns. The work of DEI still lives despite attempts to villainize it.

When the pendulum moves toward a side of justice, we will likely see shifts in DEI titles, positions, and roles again. We can simultaneously plan for today and prepare for the future, learning how to build capacity for DEI work in various seasons of our political climate. Although many position titles of today may not reflect DEI language (e.g., shifting from *Director of Equity and Inclusion* to *Director of Culture and Belonging*), I will continue to use the DEI acronym within this book as an act of resistance. DEI is also being intentionally used as the Batman 'bat signal' to summon people who occupy variations of DEI-related roles. No matter where you are or how your role has changed, *The DEI Practitioner's Handbook* should signal that this book was made out of love for you.

As you read this guidebook, you will learn about the history, complexities, and responsibilities of roles in school districts that are devised to promote and achieve equitable outcomes. You will gain knowledge of environments that are conducive for inclusionary work and learn how to combat resistance. Importantly, you will have opportunities to process your identity as a leader who is committed to educational justice. You will tap into your own humanity and reflect on your beliefs, practices, and how you show up for others. As you read this book, I highly encourage you to complete the mirror work exercises. To maintain our stamina in this work, we need intentional pauses to reflect on our leadership in isolation and with accountability partners.

Thank you for being on this journey with me. Although the world feels overwhelming at times, I take solace in knowing that there are people fighting for a world where liberation exists. Thank you for your advocacy and courage. In this era of truth decay where we are blatantly told lies and misinformation about DEI work, we need courageous leaders who are willing to stand up and fight for the educational experiences students deserve.

The work lives through us.

Acknowledgments

I wish to express my gratitude toward those who contributed to my work, well-being, and perseverance during the challenging season of writing a book in support of diversity, equity, and inclusion in an anti-DEI climate. First, I want to thank my family. When many DEI roles were being eliminated, my spouse, Jesus Rivera, encouraged me to step out on faith and conduct liberatory work on my own terms through the development of an educational consulting business. As an educational consultant, I connected with school leaders across the U.S. and internationally, gaining valuable insights into how DEI roles were leveraged in schools. Through consulting experiences, I learned many lessons about leadership and became a better practitioner for my current role in academia.

I extend my sincerest appreciation to Routledge Publishing and my editors for the opportunity to publish a second book. It has been a privilege to collaborate with Dr. Paul Gorski and Lauren Davis throughout the writing process. While many people were being discouraged from using DEI language with the introduction of new policies and executive orders, my editors encouraged me to take an authentic approach to this book. I am grateful to speak my truth during times when people are actively being silenced or censored.

The ongoing support and encouragement from my parents were greatly appreciated while writing this book. I struggled to write due to constant news coverage about the institutional rollbacks of DEI initiatives. My father regularly contacted me to monitor my progress, consistently emphasizing the importance of continuing my writing efforts. His encouragement was instrumental to me during dark times. I am grateful for my family.

When I was on the receiving end of threats, publicized attacks, and petitions against my work as a DEI practitioner, Dr. Dena Simmons reminded me of the importance of saving myself. Although we can do hard things as humans, our efforts should not cost us our mental health or livelihood. I am grateful for the clarity she brought to my life during a time when I was deeply hurt and wounded from institutions. She offered affirmations and many job postings, which empowered me to leap from an oppressive work environment.

I also want to thank all the DEI practitioners in my circles who contributed to this book—*Dr. Patricia Payne, Dr. John Marshall, Dr. Penny Robbins,*

Terri Roberts-Leonard, Joi Odom Grant, Dr. Ayva Thomas, Ranna Harb, Dr. Dwayne Chism, Dr. Renae Azziz, Dr. Dennisha Murff, and Jessica Heiser. To my friends, family members, and accountability partners, I appreciate the times you allowed me to process the dysfunction around me. Many of you were the support systems I did not have in institutions. I thank you for your wisdom, love, and responsiveness. Thank you for being a part of my community. You know who you are, and I am forever grateful.

About the Author

Dr. Erica Buchanan-Rivera (Dr. EBR) is a fierce advocate for justice-centered work and humanizing approaches in educational environments. She has served in education for nearly 20 years as a teacher, an award-winning principal, director of curriculum, and an award-winning DEI district administrator (e.g., Chief Equity and Inclusion Officer and Director of Equity and Inclusion) in suburban and urban school districts. Buchanan-Rivera's academic background includes a bachelor's degree in elementary education and a master's degree in school administration, both from Butler University where she was recognized as a Distinguished Alumni. She completed her doctoral degree from Indiana State University. Currently, Buchanan-Rivera supports aspiring K-12 and higher education leaders as an Assistant Professor at DePaul University. She also serves as an educational consultant who focuses on ideological work to support culturally responsive practices and conditions for learning.

Buchanan-Rivera has supported various universities as an adjunct professor, teaching courses that focus on pedagogical approaches, equity-focused leadership, and the intersection between the Reggio Emilia philosophy and anti-racist work. Her research centers identity-affirming environments and quantitative methods to examine inclusivity in classrooms. Her work has been featured in Education Week, Edutopia, MindShift, K-12 Dive, Educational Leadership Magazine, and many national podcasts, including *The Brown Girls Guide to Politics*. She is also the author of the book, *Identity Affirming Classrooms: Spaces that Center Humanity (2020)*. Buchanan-Rivera strives to promote school environments where students can be their authentic selves.

Introduction

We are a movement of people who choose courage and march toward freedom. We embrace our voice as a symbol of hope and a tool for change. This movement is fueled by our imaginations and visions of what the world could be. Despite oppositional forces that exist to change our course, we persist through forms of resistance. We are bound together by hope, community, and liberation, encompassing a spirit of advocacy for a different and just society. Although progress may not synchronize with our outcries for change, we recognize our power, elevate our voices, and continue to dream. We walk in truth, push for accountability, and commit to shaping the future for the next generation. We are the movement and our collective efforts are needed now more than ever.

The state of education within our current era of history compels me to think about the support systems needed for educators who lead diversity, equity, and inclusion (DEI) efforts at the school and district level. I intentionally want to shed light on the roles, responsibilities, and political landscape of DEI practitioners—*Chief Equity and Inclusion Officers, Directors of Equity and Inclusion, Racial Equity Directors,* and other people whose primary roles are focused on accountability measures for equitable systems. If you have selected this book, you are likely either in a DEI practitioner role, leading DEI work in an educational space, or considering a position to lead inclusionary efforts within a school district. My intent is to offer unfiltered truths about the delicate balance between navigating and dismantling unjust systems. I want to offer you the guidebook we did not receive upon the acceptance of our DEI roles, and share strategies, contextual examples from fellow practitioners, and pitfalls to avoid. Importantly, I want practitioners to know that they are not alone. Our frustrations, questions, and experiences are unique, yet not uncommon among a collective.

It is hard to be the light in a role that is often surrounded by political storms. Words alone cannot convey the hardships or the emotions I internalized while often being penalized for doing a job I was hired to do. In my experiences, educational leaders advocated for change within systems yet struggled to acknowledge how 'change' should include mirror work (self-examination), the elimination of racism, and approaches that embraced the humanity of all children. The more I pushed for growth in those areas, the greater the resistance. What kept me going and still propels me forward is my commitment to justice and desire to grow the next generation of changemakers. Amid executive orders and DEI rollbacks, I continue to hold on to hope because of children and the world they deserve. We must never underestimate our power or impact. We make a difference and are a critical part of this movement for liberation.

My Background as a DEI Officer

I accepted a role as a Chief Equity and Inclusion Officer following the completion of my doctoral degree. Prior to accepting the position, I had served as a kindergarten teacher, a principal (in two different schools), and a K-12 director of curriculum. Through my work in those positions, I developed extensive expertise in chairing committees and overseeing projects centered on diversity, equity, and inclusion. My doctoral research was an instrumentation method where I developed a tool to measure inclusion in classroom environments. I was passionate about creating affirming educational spaces as a result of my own school experiences where I often felt marginalized because of my Blackness. Therefore, it was a full circle moment to take on a role where I could focus on the creation and sustainability of culturally responsive environments. It was a role that not only embodied my scholarship, but welcomed my identities and histories as an integral part of my labor.

The district where I accepted my first DEI position was high-performing and located in a predominantly white, suburban community outside of Indianapolis, Indiana. My role was grant-funded, which necessitated adherence to defined metrics and expectations as stipulated by funding guidelines. I focused my efforts on building trust and a common, shared language for equitable practices. Through discussions and insights from staff, students, and families, I gained knowledge of the foundational work that was needed to improve systems. I was energized by the possibilities and challenging tasks ahead. Yet, when it was a time to do the actual work, it did not take long to realize that my mission was misaligned with the expectations of school board members and people within the community.

Despite ongoing opposition, I worked hard to build capacity and systems to support inclusionary work. I devised consistent professional learning opportunities, affinity spaces for students and staff, community coalitions, and partnerships to advance equity. Nevertheless, my efforts were not promoted or made visible by the district leaders, which was a choice. As the first Chief Equity and Inclusion Officer and Black woman in a cabinet-level position, I often felt silenced and suffocated by racial microaggressions. A sector of the community did everything in their power to protect a status quo that upheld white supremacy. White parents feared that messages of educational justice meant indoctrination or negligence of their children's needs, while some parents from other racialized groups made it clear that my work harmed their elite positioning within the community. *I'm a Black physician who is financially stable, works hard, and has earned respect, oppression does not exist.* Board members also initiated intimidation tactics, often leaving anti-DEI pamphlets in my office mailbox to 'educate' me.

My words of advocacy within the institution started to land in conservative articles, right-leaning social media platforms, and radio shows that elicited online, anonymous threats. Facing opposition for affirming all children was difficult, particularly without workplace support. District leadership could have shaped the narrative by communicating the benefits of inclusion and equity for all students but remained silent as misinformation spread, making me the martyr. During an evening where I wrestled with many emotions, my friend, Dena Simmons called to remind me that "sometimes you have to save yourself." When you work in an environment where you lack trust or protection, it may be time for a necessary ending.

I resigned from that school corporation nearly three years later to become the first Director of Equity and Inclusion in an urban district. This role included responsibilities similar to my previous position, but also entailed many other areas of oversight including K-12 high ability systems, social workers, and social emotional learning (SEL). I worked with a supportive school board and felt empowered to lead change with a collaborative team. There was a collective response to resistance, especially during the rise of anti-CRT (Critical Race Theory) legislation where all district leaders denounced censorship bills. However, leadership dynamics and methods to support achievement were often a point of contention.

Following a reorganization of roles, I felt led to focus on my consulting work and growing leaders through higher education. It has been liberating to have the world as a classroom while serving as a consultant, and I value teaching aspiring principals, superintendents, and higher education leaders as an Assistant Professor of educational leadership. The lessons I have learned from DEI practitioner roles have shaped how I engage in educational experiences and have ultimately made me a better human.

Being the First

When we commit to being the first in a newly created role, there is no blueprint for our daily operations. We are positioned to build our own systems, communication channels, and metrics to assess our work. There is pressure to demonstrate our relevance in organizations where people do not fully understand our roles. It can also feel isolating to work in a position where no one shares similar responsibilities, leaving us to find accountability partners or perhaps, collaboration outside of the workplace.

Most of the jobs I have held in education were the 'first' for an organization. I was not only entering newly established roles within school districts but also broke ground as the first Black woman to hold those positions. Being the first Black woman in educational leadership positions added another layer of complexity on top of job responsibilities. While working in a predominantly white field, and particularly in predominantly white communities, I have encountered unchecked racial biases, microaggressions, and scenarios where my credentials have been challenged. There were times when I was labeled as 'angry' for expressing my thoughts in a straightforward manner. Meanwhile, if white colleagues expressed the same thoughts with profanity, they were either noted as admirable or comical in the moment. It can feel heavy when your work, language, and movements are under scrutiny by individuals who have not engaged in introspective work to examine their preconceived notions about race.

For those who identify as Black, Indigenous, Asian, Latinx, or a person of color, we must consider job expectations and the hazards from working in environments that lack culturally responsive practices and uphold whiteness (i.e., white ways of being as a standard). In predominantly white institutions (PWIs), it may be challenging to feel validated, allyship, or heard unless intentional strategies are utilized among leaders to build trust and authentic relationships. This includes the strategy of having the hard, necessary conversations about race. When I hear announcements that an individual will be the first person of color within a role, I celebrate while knowing the taxing journey ahead. Being the first comes with costs that must be considered and named long before signing a contract.

Although there are downsides to being the first, not all experiences are catastrophic or lead to harmful outcomes. If positioned in conditions that are conducive for justice-centered work, being the first could lead to the implementation of innovative ideas that transform systems and generate positive outcomes for students. Our creative genius can lead to collective efforts that improve instructional practices, policies, and school climates for students, staff, and families. I have proudly spearheaded policy changes, student leadership conferences, community-based organizations, and learning experiences that have been impactful 'firsts' for school districts. Many of those firsts were developed within oppressive systems. It is possible to push, build a movement, and create something beautiful when the odds are against you. Being first means that we are a part of a living history, where we can potentially build a legacy that inspires others.

Leading for Humanity and Justice in Unjust Systems

We have seen many shifts in our political climate over the last few years. The global pandemic fragmented many communities. There were people who embraced science and the severity of COVID-19, while others refused to acknowledge its existence. As I drove to work, "Unmask our Kids" signs were posted near major intersections. Many families, including my own, experienced loss of life and could not fully honor their loved ones due to funeral home restrictions. During the onset of the pandemic, we also learned about the tragic murders of Ahmaud Arbery and Breonna Taylor. Then, the world was exposed to Derek Chauvin kneeling on George Floyd's neck for 9 minutes and 29 seconds (Bogel-Burroughs, 2021).

The national response to George Floyd's murder was an ephemeral racial reckoning I had not seen before in my lifetime. Books that discussed the origin of racism and anti-racist education became bestsellers. Scholars who were experts in racial equity research were centered on prime-time television. Protests against police brutality were conducted in major cities across the country. Community learning in the form of book studies and local events emerged. Numerous organizations crafted commitment statements in support of Black lives, and launched DEI-related positions. When DEI work became profitable, there was also a rise in new anti-racist organizations and consultants, many with little to no experience. As a racial equity scholar, this was the first time many white colleagues and friends reached out to have personal and raw conversations about race.

Less than a year later, I was reminded of bell hooks' (2001) words that radical changes lead to citizens of our nation betraying their hearts. Our democracy was threatened via a violent insurrection at the U.S. Capitol followed by a rise in curriculum censorship laws, book banning, gun violence, and policies rooted in transphobia. Books that were celebrated for igniting discussions about racism were scrutinized and shoveled through school-based complaint processes. DEI-focused positions that were heavily prevalent in corporate offices were slowly eradicated as thousands were laid off (Chen & Weber, 2023). Some states, including Florida, Texas, and Oklahoma, codified the removal of DEI departments in educational institutions (Walker, 2023). Although policies and people in positions of power have created barriers for liberatory work, educational leaders and service-based organizations are still challenged to create institutional cultures that generate a sense of belonging.

We know that the happenings in the world influence actions and outcomes in educational environments. From legislation pertaining to curriculum censorship to reading instruction and how we acknowledge students' gender identities, we recognize the impact society has on school policies and culture. It feels heavy at times to exist on a living Jumanji board known as our sociopolitical climate. Yet, we must remind ourselves that dehumanization, colonization, and harmful government-sanctioned policies are the origin story of many countries. Nonetheless, history has also demonstrated generations of activists using their collective will and power to combat unjust systems. Throughout past and present history there are stories of resistance, grassroots movements, and youth advocacy that remind us how dreams of liberation can come to life.

When Florida's Board of Education approved new K-12 guidelines for Black history curriculum and eliminated advanced placement (AP) African American Studies courses (Modan, 2023) faith leaders from Black churches organized to teach Black history lessons within their communities (Powell, 2024). Reverend Rhonda Thomas, who leads an organization called "Faith in Florida," developed a history toolkit for churches that is accessed across approximately 29 states in nearly 400 houses of worship. Following anti-DEI executive orders within the United States, I was also inspired by an interview (Singer, 2025) that featured Faustina Cuevas, a DEI officer and coalition chair in Massachusetts. When questioned about the impact of executive orders on the actions of municipal leaders committed to advancing diversity, equity, and inclusion, Cuevas stated "We are steadfast on doing what we've got to do on the ground … Whatever is coming out of Washington, we're just going to keep full steam ahead."

Racism, bigotry, and deficit ideologies cemented into laws do not eliminate our capacity to show up for humanity. We may have to reimagine the implementation of our work and the language we use to define it while under political scrutiny or dictatorships, but it does not stop our ability to advocate for just outcomes. Despite political tides, we can use our voice and push for change. We can transfer our rage into productivity and mobilize others to make a difference. Through innovation and intentionality in our strategic planning, we can remove barriers and structures that perpetuate oppressive conditions. There is power in community, and together we can deliberately act to challenge abused power, inequitable systems, and fascism.

For the Love of You

My career of teaching, leading, and consulting in education has gifted me with many human connections. I am grateful to be in circles with a myriad of teachers and educational leaders, across the U.S. and internationally, who are doing impactful work. Through these human interactions, I have acquired many stories and outcries for change related to the state of education. When people share their truths, I accept the role of being a mindful listener and respect people's requests to refrain from action or to maintain confidentiality. (*I am only venting, please don't tell anyone or do anything about it.*) If my body was a technology device, my storage space would likely be maxed out and I would receive internal alerts to delete information. Yet, in all seriousness, the ongoing consumption of peoples' grievances and desires for justice while existing in an anti-DEI political climate, constantly leaves me in a state of rage.

> *I am angry that many teachers feel isolated in the workplace for their commitment to culturally responsive teaching practices.*
>
> *I have anger toward educational leaders who allow community members to bully teachers into leaving their schools or the profession due to accusations of 'wokeness' or indoctrinating students.*
>
> *I am angry by the number of recommendations I have written for teachers in efforts to help them leave toxic work cultures that were resistant to inclusionary practices yet open to discrimination.*
>
> *I am angry that many educational leaders abandoned efforts to promote diversity, equity, or inclusion long before executive orders—or were relieved to let go of commitments as a result of anti-DEI policies.*
>
> *I am angry by the number of teachers of color who experience racism, hostility, and racial microaggressions in the workplace, while being asked or appointed to work on committees that focus on inclusive environments for students and families.*
>
> *I am angry about the disconnect between mission statements and accountability systems within various schools.*
>
> *I have anger toward educational leaders who 'talk the talk' while their leadership actions hinder equitable practices and cause staff turnover.*
>
> *I am angry by the number of families and students who continue to experience educational malpractices.*
>
> *I am angry … and challenged to find productive ways to channel my rage every day.*

Toni Morrison (1987) stated in an interview that anger is paralyzing and emphasized the need to focus on our power and skills. Black women scholars and activists, Audre Lorde and bell hooks, have also taught me that rage can be used as a tool and a force to evoke transformative work.

Rather than wallowing in our anger, we can use it to organize collective efforts and advocate for just systems. Mary Rice-Boothe (2023) the author of *Leading within Systems of Inequity in Education: A Liberation Guide for Leaders of Color*, discusses the importance of practicing love and rage. She conveys how rage can be a catalyst for leading with love and directing our focus on what matters. We can channel our anger to focus on justice and our love for humanity. Toni Morrison's words hold truth that we can get angry and then go to work.

This book is my anger redirected as a body of love for all who uphold freedom dreams in a broken world. I want us to thrive, lead with courage, and prioritize our wellness. My heart desires for us to work in inviting spaces where people value our intellect and contributions. Out of love, I offer guidance for the examination of systems and the acceleration of mirror work within schools. I need our colleagues to see themselves and to engage in introspective work to become better practitioners and accomplices. No matter the obstacle or forces of opposition, you are not alone. The movement of liberatory work is love in action and rooted in community. We do not have to operate in isolation and are stronger together.

Guiding Principles for Leading Liberatory Work

This book aims to support any educator who is in a leadership position to advance and promote diversity, equity, and inclusion (e.g., teacher leader, coach, director, assistant superintendent, officer etc.). I refer to these positions as DEI practitioners within the book, yet recognize that each role may carry a unique title that does not reflect the acronym. Importantly, I want to note that I am using the acronym, DEI, rather than listing the words diversity, equity, and inclusion. I recognize that it is important to name diversity, equity, and inclusion to avoid the weaponization of the terms, and I challenge people to unpack the meaning of each word in my work as a practitioner. However, for the purpose of being concise in this text, I will refer to diversity, equity, and inclusion as the acronym, DEI.

The following guiding principles are woven throughout the book to empower you to lead for equitable outcomes:

Release the notion that you are solely responsible for transforming systems of injustice. Yes, I am shouting this through a megaphone to ensure the message is clear. You are not the savior, fixer, emancipator, or the Olivia Pope of an institution. You are not going to unravel structural and institutional inequalities with deep historical roots by yourself. This work is done in community with others. Accountability should extend to all who are employed within an organization and operating within systems. We can lead, provide resources and support, educate, and engage in problem-solving processes, but outcomes should not rely on the brilliance of one individual.

Environment matters. As practitioners in pursuit of equitable practices, it is necessary for us to consider where our efforts will thrive. Not all spaces will embrace our gifts, voice, or recommendations for change. We must consider if we are positioned in educational environments that are conducive for change and a disruption of the status quo. We do not have to stay in a space that makes us a billboard for inclusion, while implementing exclusionary practices.

Be a critical examiner of the institution you serve, and importantly, yourself. While analyzing school systems (e.g., instructional, transportation, technology, student services, health and wellness, etc.), it is necessary to question practices and study outcomes. Who benefits from systems? Who is harmed by systems? We must understand what perpetuates and sustains injustice within systems. While using our voice, leading departments, and making decisions, we must look deeply at our own humanity. Thich Nhat Hanh (1991) reminds us that "we have to look deeply at things in order to see (p. 104)." When leading for humanity, it is critical for us to see how we have been shaped to view the world, systems, and the humanity of others.

Walk in your values. Leadership is a range of behaviors based on our values. If we value relationships or effective communication, then our behaviors should align with relational skills that yield to connectivity. When we walk in our values, we live out our rhetoric and beliefs. We have a clear understanding of who we are, what we stand for, and what we are against. Walking in our values means that we practice our beliefs in the face of resistance. We do not alter ourselves or compromise who we are to have a place within an institution.

Commit to learning and unlearning. We may be positioned as an 'expert' or the go-to person within our school district or building, but we are whole humans who require life-long learning. We need time to nurture our genius, and we deepen our knowledge from human connections. There will also be times when we must admit that we don't have the answers or that our assessments are inaccurate. We all require growth for human development and will unlearn things as a result of new information. Therefore, let's give ourselves grace while riding the rollercoaster known as life.

Protect your peace, seek joy, and give yourself flowers. We exist in a climate where many politicians or political groups have prioritized the demise of DEI efforts over the welfare of humanity. There are times when headlines and political unrest can impact our wellness. Sometimes, we may need to walk away from sources of stress to protect our peace and seek restoration. It is important to affirm ourselves and embrace self-love, since we cannot always count on institutions or other people to give us the flowers or care we deserve.

Tap into the wisdom of ancestors. DEI practitioner roles and positions would not be possible without the will and strength of freedom fighters before us. Although most institutions do not provide a guidebook for liberatory work, the playbook already exists. Activist and SNCC founder Ella Baker taught me the art of grassroots movements and community empowerment. Annie Pearl Avery, member of SNCC and fierce advocate for voting rights, embraced me in a literal hug during a random encounter in Selma, AL, and emphasized how I needed to be fearless and push limits to obtain freedom. Paulo Freire and James Baldwin, both activists and writers, elevated my critical consciousness. Abolitionist Angela Davis instilled the power of radicalizing my mind and reimagining systems beyond the confines of oppressive structures. There are many parallels between the freedom struggles of the past and liberation movements of the present. We have much to learn from those who have paved the way for civil and human rights.

The Shaping of this Book

Chapter 1 provides historical and political contexts surrounding work that promotes DEI. Terminology is defined and actions are interrogated, including the unintended harm of DEI efforts when executed ineffectively by school leaders. There are practitioners who are more focused on managing inequities and controlling a narrative (that favors an institution), rather than eradicating barriers and institutional oppression—*and in some cases, hands are tied.* It is necessary to discuss how we can be a part of the problem.

Chapter 2 discusses the roles and responsibilities of DEI practitioners, including misconceptions and pitfalls to avoid. Chapter 3 supports practitioners in pursuit of DEI leadership roles. It describes what job candidates should look for in an institution that is committed to educational justice. For those who are currently in DEI-related positions, this chapter could either be affirming or signal professional shifts that need to be made for your growth or wellness. Chapter 4 conveys how we build capacity and effective strategies at the systems level, while Chapter 5 focuses on efforts to foster an inclusive work culture.

Chapter 6 explores the work of creating school environments that are free of harassment and discrimination. It discusses the responsibilities of DEI practitioners who manage policies and oversee guidelines pertaining to Title IX, Title VI, and the ADA. Many DEI practitioners also act as Title IX coordinators at a school or district level. I have served as a Title IX and Title VI coordinator, handling investigations regarding discrimination. These areas of law are constantly evolving, which is why I included an attorney's perspective in this chapter (who graciously reviewed the chapter as well). There are proactive strategies and processes that can be implemented to create environments free of harassment and discrimination.

Chapter 7, the last and final section of the book, illuminates the protection of one's peace and how to navigate resistance. Research consistently demonstrates how the manifestation of unresolved stress can lead to physical and mental health concerns. We need to consider the mental preparation that is needed for moments of adversity and determine our response to backlash from our efforts. Most chapters will also include personal narratives or accounts from fellow DEI practitioners. No one is alone in this work, and it is affirming when we can see ourselves in others' stories.

Following the chapters, there are tools including a letter to district superintendents who oversee DEI roles. This would be a great letter to share with your school boards or executive leadership teams within a district. I recognize that leaders who choose to employ a DEI specialist or someone dedicated to advancing inclusive practices are motivated by positive intentions. A need is evident, and a position is approved to address the need. Nevertheless, some leaders do not recognize nor understand the conditions needed to support the effectiveness of DEI practitioners. When executive leaders do not fully understand DEI work, they may unintentionally hinder efforts toward equitable outcomes.

Educator activism has been prevalent in school spaces long before the development of positions that included terms such as equity, inclusion, or belonging. DEI has also been in existence *and controversial* long before recent, copycat legislation across countries. The work of creating just school environments and the fight for basic human rights has been intergenerational labor. The upcoming chapter helps us to understand the purpose of DEI and the complexities of roles that are designed to advance equity. We need to learn about the political and historical landscapes of DEI work.

References

Bogel-Burroughs, N. (2021, March 30). Prosecutors say Derek Chauvin knelt on George Floyd for 9 minutes 29 seconds, longer than initially reported. The New York Times. https://www.nytimes.com/2021/03/30/us/derek-chauvin-george-floyd-kneel-9-minutes-29-seconds.html

Chen, T.-P., & Weber, L. (2023, July 21). The rise and fall of the chief diversity officer—WSJ. The Wall Street Journal. https://www.wsj.com/articles/chief-diversity-officer-cdo-business-corporations-e110a82f

Hanh, T. N. (1991). *Peace is every step*. Bantam Books.

hooks, b. (2021). *All about love: New visions*. William Morrow, an imprint of HarperCollins Publishers.

Modan, N. (2023, July 20). Florida approves controversial African American history Standards. K12 Dive. https://www.k12dive.com/news/florida-approves-divisive-african-american-history-standards-amid-controver/688526/

Morrison, T. (1987, September 15). Interview by Don Swam, CBS.

Powell, H. (2024, February 19). Black churches in Florida step in to teach Black history amid restrictions. The Christian Broadcasting Network. https://cbn.com/news/us/black-churches-florida-step-teach-black-history-amid-restrictions

Rice-Boothe, M. (2023). *Leading within systems of inequity in education: A liberation guide for leaders of color*. ASCD.

Singer, P. (2025, January 24). Mass. cities and towns stay committed to DEI despite Trump's federal order. https://www.wgbh.org/news/local/2025-01-24/mass-cities-and-towns-stay-committed-to-dei-despite-trumps-federal-order

Walker, A. (2023, December 14). Oklahoma governor signs order effectively banning diversity programs at public colleges. The Guardian. https://www.theguardian.com/us-news/2023/dec/14/oklahoma-ban-diversity-dei-program-colleges

1

Understanding the History and Complexities of DEI Work

The field of diversity, equity, and inclusion (DEI) is layered with complexities, unwavering opposition, and an extensive history of activism. Prior to discussing the roles and responsibilities of DEI practitioners, the language of liberatory work needs to be defined. Dwayne Chism (2022), author of *Leading Your School Toward Equity* states, "when equity remains undefined or vaguely understood in an organization, focusing on it tends to build a culture of opposition (p. 15)." When coherence of DEI terminology is absent, people will use their personal interpretations and lack of knowledge as weapons to hinder just outcomes. Misconceptions about DEI create confusion over the purpose and impact of DEI roles in education. It is crucial to understand the historical context of positions dedicated to DEI; to consider the political environment surrounding DEI roles; and to clarify the terminology that defines our work.

Exploring Diversity, Equity, and Inclusion

Diversity, equity, and inclusion are interconnected concepts with distinct meanings. While working with other humans, we note specific characteristics, abilities, features, and beliefs that enable us to differentiate. In the most simplistic terms, diversity means differences. As educational leaders, we are challenged to consider how we support and acknowledge the wide array of lived experiences, identities, and cultures that intertwine to breathe life into the systems we operate in daily, particularly schools. An appreciation for diversity

DOI: 10.4324/9781032623542-1

means that we recognize the value (e.g., gifts, beauty, strengths, etc.) of each person and their human condition. We see ourselves as imperfect beings who process, communicate, and respond in varied ways. The ability to recognize differences and the humanity of others needs to be uplifted in our approaches and the lenses we carry into our endeavors and interpersonal relationships.

Mirror work challenges us to explore the shaping of our humanity. Through studying the construction of self, we can learn how we have been socialized to view and respond to differences. We have all formulated favorable or negative opinions about people or environments because of internalized messaging from society. Part of our mirror work is recognizing our behaviors in social contexts and processing the origin of our thought patterns. We must purposely consider the intersections of our identities (e.g., race, geographical location, religion, gender, etc.) and how elements of 'self' shape our perception of others. This reflection of our social conditioning should also include the beliefs that activate the specious categorizations we adhere to individuals or groups of people.

Diversity also references the differences that are prevalent in one's navigation within systems. The categorizations humans develop from biases, binary thinking, and deficit ideologies work in tandem to generate oppressive conditions, systems, and environments. Through the scholarship of Kimberlé Crenshaw (1989) and Patricia Collins (2015), intersectionality is defined as an analysis of power that describes the relationship between overlapping identities and systems of inequity. Our positioning within society is influenced by our overlapping identities. We must recognize that multiple people can operate within the same system and leave with different experiences or outcomes. Inequitable outcomes are rooted in how people are treated differently by systems based on their identities.

Educational equity is often referenced as the concept of giving individuals what they need to thrive. However, I find that definition to be vague and open to weaponization. I have seen educators employ punitive policies or practices in the spirit of giving a student what they believed was needed. *He (student) needed to be punished through public humiliation, it's the only way he will learn to do better*. Therefore, I prefer to define educational equity as a conceptualization of the following:

1 Educational equity is the recognition of how power generates imbalances in educational systems.
2 Educational equity describes how we use our power to create just systems and eliminate barriers to support student outcomes.
3 Educational equity is the work of shifting power to historically marginalized and underserved communities to increase access, opportunities, and to foster advancement.

Equity is about power (Buchanan-Rivera, 2022). It is understanding the role of power and how it is used to either dismantle or contribute to the widening of disparities. Our perspectives on equity are inherently linked to our underlying beliefs about diversity. Beliefs and values can materialize into structures that either liberate or oppress others when coupled with power. If we believe that certain communities or individuals are not worthy of basic human rights, then our actions and decision-making will be prone to dehumanizing practices. We have witnessed the aftermath of politicians, board members, and executive leaders who have brought their anti-Black or anti-immigrant ideologies to fruition with the use of power. We have seen headlines featuring the terrorization of ICE raids on campuses and neighborhoods stemming from dehumanizing, racist beliefs. Equity-focused principles require us to examine our beliefs, power, and actions. We use our power to show up for humanity through the elimination of discriminatory practices and barriers, ensuring that people can thrive within environments regardless of their background.

Inclusion alludes to the meaningful practices that encourage individuals to show up as their authentic selves. It is the intentional work of being responsive to diversity. An inclusive culture embodies acceptance and solidarity. There are other existing acronyms that are an expansion of DEI, including ones that add justice (DEIJ), belonging (DEIJB), or accessibility (DEIA). DEI practitioner job titles may include a combination of these terms or have a specific area of focus, such as racial justice. As a result of anti-DEI policies, many positions have also shifted to titles that incorporate the term belonging (e.g., Director of Belonging, Director of Inclusion and Belonging, etc.), which focuses on the human experience and connectivity. People can be invited to the table and included in opportunities while simultaneously experiencing exclusion. Therefore, titles that include belonging or culture emphasize organizational efforts that foster connections and trusting relationships.

If you have ever watched Charlie Brown's Thanksgiving special (1973), you will understand the difference between inclusion and belonging through the experience of the only Black character, Franklin. In response to the Civil Rights movement, cartoonist Charles Schulz created Franklin, who was the first Black character in the Peanuts comic strip (Amatangelo, 2024). While Franklin was intended to symbolize inclusion and advancements in racial equality, the film depicted him seated separately from white characters during the Thanksgiving meal. From experience, I know that DEI practitioners can also be positioned as the 'Franklin' within institutions. In other words, we may be invited to the table (e.g., meetings, events, leadership gatherings, etc.) but lack authentic connections, power, or the support needed to belong or feel valued.

In the book, *Belonging* (2009), bell hooks conveyed that "communities of care are sustained by rituals of regard (p. 229)." A culture of high regard for humans involves the work of active listening, affirming strengths, and being responsive to diverse needs. We all deserve environments where people value our voices and contributions. We all deserve workspaces where leaders engage in ethical decision-making and embrace an anti-biased approach. We all deserve a community of care and practices that demonstrate respect for human dignity. When belonging, inclusion, equity, and other justice-centered language are clearly defined, internalized, experienced, and living in systems, it becomes harder for oppositional groups to use DEI as a political tool to stoke fear and division—*a playbook that has strategically been leveraged with a high success rate in many parts of our world.*

Emergence of DEI Officers

The separate but equal doctrine was dismantled after the ruling of the *Brown vs. Board of Education* (1954). It was declared that segregated educational facilities were unconstitutional as well as a violation of the Fourteenth Amendment. Although the ruling produced social and political polarization, it also led to many social movements (Minow, 2010). The Civil Rights Act of 1964 ended segregation in public facilities, enforced the right to vote, and outlawed discrimination on the basis of race, color, religion, sex, or national origin (Title VII). As a part of the law's provision, the Equal Employment Opportunity Commission (EEOC) was established to address employment discrimination (EEOC, 2024). Through the EEOC, roles such as Affirmative Action Officers were established to maintain legal compliance and anti-discrimination.

The protection of civil rights continued with the passing of the Bilingual Education Act in 1968 to support multilingual learners in schools (Urban & Wagoner, 2014). Disability activists also mobilized in the 1960s to advocate for civil rights among disabled communities. The Rehabilitation Act of 1973 prohibited discrimination on the basis of cognitive or physical disabilities. By 1990, the Individual with Disabilities Education Act (IDEA) was established to not only promote inclusion in school settings but also to include the importance of parental rights.

Congress enacted Title IX of the Education Amendments of 1972 (Boschert, 2022). Title IX was authorized to ban discrimination on the basis of sex in schools, educational programs, or activities that receive federal funding. This area of law and its regulations continue to evolve and determine the measures Title IX Coordinators implement in educational settings. The Age Discrimination Act of 1975 ensured that individuals would not be excluded from programs or activities that also received federal financial assistance based on age (U.S. Department of Labor). However, the law did not apply to employment matters, which were handled through processes under the EEOC. Several laws were enacted after the Civil Rights Act to ensure students had equal access to education.

Chief Equity Officer positions emerged as a branch of Title VII of the Civil Rights Act. The roles were positioned within the federal government (TRIO programs) and expanded to various industries, including education. DEI practitioner roles were ubiquitous in higher education and private sectors but steadily increased in public K-12 school environments in 2020 (Rice-Boothe, 2023). School leaders, particularly DEI practitioners, are responsible for safeguarding the civil and human rights of students. These roles were developed with the intent to create and maintain environments free of harassment and discrimination. However, the degree of power practitioners have to develop proactive measures and transform systems varies across contexts.

Political backlash, anti-DEI policies, and economic downturns have compelled many organizations to eliminate or restructure DEI departments. Restructuring may look like changes in terminology, shifting a position title from *Director of Equity and Inclusion* to *Director of Culture and Community Relations*, or scrubbing DEI-related language from websites to replace words (e.g., diversity, equity, and inclusion) with terms that lack criticism (e.g., differences, culture, belonging, community, partnerships, merit, etc.). Other shifts may include the reorganization of job responsibilities for DEI practitioners or changes in evaluative metrics. For instance, Human Resource (HR) departments may embed DEI initiatives into their operations, measuring employee retention as opposed to evaluating hiring practices and the diversification of staff. No matter the structure, title change, or governmental policy, we are still here and committed to generating the environments students deserve.

The Controversy Surrounding DEI Work

The concepts of DEI have garnered national criticism, resulting in strategic, well-funded campaigns and policies to remove initiatives, professions, and departments related to inclusionary work. Conservative policymakers have pushed back against efforts to diversify institutions (i.e., striking affirmative action) and programs, and deem the promotion of belonging and racial equity as a discriminatory practice. We have witnessed lawmakers' promotion of curriculum censorship bills and whitewashed curricular materials to make slavery look like a mentorship program rather than a dehumanizing experience.

Prior to the Trump administration's executive orders to terminate DEI programs in the federal government (removing federal grants tied to DEI initiatives), there were studies conducted that demonstrated the power of anti-DEI campaigns on legislative branches.

The Chronicle of Higher Education conducted a study and reported in 2023 that 40 bills were introduced in 22 states to restrict or eliminate DEI programming in public colleges. Paulette Granberry Russell (Wood, 2023), the former president of the National Association of Diversity Officers in Higher Education, stated that Supreme Court outcomes and ongoing legislative decisions were "dismantling at least 50 years of incremental progress, slow progress in addressing the needs of diverse students in higher education" prior to executive orders.

Similar trends were noted in K-12 environments as a result of conservatives' strategic focus on critical race theory (CRT). Virtually, no K-12 educators were teaching CRT tenets in classroom environments. However, it was easier for politicians to villainize the acronym, CRT, rather than the term 'diversity' or personalized stories about the permanence of racism. The 'CRT Forward Initiative' from UCLA's Critical Race Studies (CRS) program conveyed in a national report (Reinhard, 2023) that lawmakers enacted anti-CRT policies in over 25 states in K-12 institutions. Over 70% of the policies focused on curriculum censorship and the pedagogical approaches or behaviors of teachers (controlling the 'radical' teacher). The enacted anti-CRT measures impacted over 22 million children within the US and continue to rise with the addition of executive orders. Political movements and policies that challenge DEI initiatives require us to adopt strategic approaches, ensuring the well-being of students and staff.

Why DEI Strikes a Chord with Advocates of Justice

We know that ideologies influence the perceptions people carry about one's humanity. Therefore, I would expect someone who upholds bigotry or anti-Black ideologies to be at the forefront of attempts to erase my rights and existence as a Black woman. However, we also need to address the elephant in the room and examine the ways DEI has failed those who believe in its principles.

To be honest, I was initially afraid to write a book that explored roles and concepts related to DEI. The world was imploding, positions were disappearing, and many people within my circles were experiencing harm from poorly executed DEI initiatives. When educational leaders leap into action without engaging themselves or employees in mirror work, DEI initiatives can be harmful and ineffective. While writing this book amid ongoing violence in Gaza, I have worked with Palestinian and Jewish educators who claim that their identities are discounted in DEI-related conversations. There have been Palestinian educators (and children) who have felt physically and emotionally unsafe as a result of pro-Israel statements released from schools (*as opposed to school officials acknowledging the pain of both communities and providing resources to support all children*). Meanwhile, the Anti-Defamation League (Chavez,

2024) reported a 361% increase in antisemitic incidents following the terrorist actions of Hamas. Jewish colleagues and close friends (who actively make an effort to interrogate whiteness in Jewish communities and are strong allies) have indicated that the work of addressing antisemitism is rarely included in school-based DEI efforts. Palestinian educators have echoed the similar sentiments about Islamophobia and have shared stories of repercussions received in the workplace for advocacy toward their communities. When DEI efforts become selective in nature and dictate what causes people should elevate, there will be communities that do not see their humanity reflected in educational leaders' interpretations of liberatory work.

Dwayne Chism (2022) also conveys that DEI efforts fall short when the focus is on compliance rather than the conditions needed for continuous improvement. For example, completion rates from a professional development experience are valuable data points, but knowing who attended a workshop does not sustain learning, nor does it foster a culture of accountability. There are many equity-related initiatives implemented for people to say *I did it* as opposed to *I learned from it and know how to use it in my practice.* Furthermore, Chism discusses how the desire to protect staff morale can sometimes serve as a barrier to the creation of equitable environments. In *Avoiding Racial Equity Detours,* Paul Gorski (2019) referenced the protection of morale as the 'pacing-for-privilege' detour. Oftentimes, school leaders prioritize the comfort of people who do not align with DEI efforts, catering to whiteness. Bettina Love's bestselling book, *Punished for Dreaming,* continues this line of thought and states that *DEI work coddles whiteness, is race-evasive, and upholds white supremacy* (2023, p. 235). When educational staff are invested in freedom and leadership is invested in protecting the emotions of bigots, DEI becomes a facade that holds no value.

There are many other criticisms of DEI work from those who are genuinely concerned about the well-being of all children and outcomes of racialized or intentionally marginalized communities. The following list includes valid critiques of DEI work and roles in educational settings based on professional listening tours:

- **Awareness-focused, no actions:** DEI work that lacks intentionality, focuses on awareness of educational injustice and not a commitment to actions. More talk, less doing.
- **Optics:** DEI may be noted as a selling point to attract families within school districts, but it does not live within buildings or the actions of leaders. Inclusion and belonging are promoted, not experienced.
- **Absence of accountability:** DEI may lack accountability measures or progress monitoring within school systems. Oftentimes, educators

of color and equity-minded practitioners are positioned to do the heavy-lifting of DEI work while not having the power to hold others accountable. No accountability, no priority.

- **No visibility of efforts:** DEI efforts are led within districts, yet faculty, staff, and teachers may not be aware of goals, strategies, or what equity means. No visibility, no evidence of efforts.
- **Lack of support systems:** DEI practitioners are likely to report to a power dynamic that lacks knowledge of their responsibilities and the will to change the status quo. Hard work, little to no support.

From selective social justice causes to the protection of whiteness and failed methods of implementation, I can empathize with people who have dissociated from DEI. I also know there are bad actors who take on roles as resume-builders with no true investment in the real work that is needed to eliminate inequities. During my tenure as a DEI officer, I engaged with plenty of people who did not initially give me a chance and thought I was tap dancing for white supremacy. If you have experienced these sentiments prior to the implosion of DEI initiatives in our political climate (as I recognize many practitioners' hands are currently tied to avoid funding cuts), please know that I hear you and wholeheartedly understand your frustrations. As the pendulum shifts and hopefully leans toward the side of justice, these are the areas that need to be addressed to make DEI more purposeful and impactful. I would be remiss to write a book that ignores the harm people have experienced in the name of DEI, and my intent is to address barriers and revive hope. We need to restore the potential of these roles and find ways to march forward.

How Do We Move Forward?

In the next few chapters, I will discuss the responsibilities, environments, and systems work of DEI practitioners. I realize that the names of positions and titles may have changed for practitioners, yet for the purpose of building community and reclaiming power over a term that's been weaponized, I will continue to use the term DEI as an act of resistance. The guidelines shared in this book are informed by research, years of experience, and reflect what DEI could be within schools. Based on the number of students and school families who are an integral part of my life, I understand firsthand how powerful these positions can be when they incorporate humanizing approaches. The harms people have experienced from DEI are real and reveal that systems need to be challenged. Effective DEI work requires a focus on the conditions that encourage collective approaches and the disruption of inequities. These conditions will be explored, including the environments where this work can thrive.

Chapter Highlights

1. When concepts related to diversity, equity, and inclusion are coherent, understood, and practiced, it becomes harder for people to weaponize what is living and operating within systems.
2. Do not believe the masses who celebrate the downfall of DEI. The terminology continues to live in systems and influences institutional practices, decision-making, and human interactions. *We are still here. We are still fighting. We still believe we can make a difference.*
3. The controversy surrounding DEI comes from all sides of the political spectrum. We must understand the unintended harm of DEI—*especially when efforts are executed poorly*—and focus on the conditions that yield to just environments.

Mirror Work

1. How would you assess your advocacy in relation to educational justice?
2. Consider your beliefs about diversity, equity, inclusion, belonging, and accessibility. Reflect on where these concepts live in your life (Figure 1.1).

Where Does Liberatory Work Live in Your Life?			
	What does this concept mean to you?	**Where do you see this concept live within workspaces?**	**Where does this concept live within your everyday life?**
Diversity			
Equity			
Inclusion			
Belonging			
Accessibility			

Figure 1.1 Where does liberatory work live in your life?

3 What are your personal critiques about DEI work? What would you do differently?
4 What propels you to move forward, grow, and embrace the journey as a DEI practitioner?

References

Amatangelo, A. (2024, February 15). *"'Welcome home, Franklin' tells backstory of the first Black 'Peanuts' character."* Los Angeles Times. https://www.latimes.com/entertainment-arts/tv/story/2024-02-15/snoopy-presents-welcome-home-franklin-robb-armstrong

Boschert, S. (2022). *37 Words: Title IX and fifty years of fighting sex discrimination*. The New Press.

Buchanan-Rivera, E. (2022). *Identity affirming classrooms: Spaces that center humanity*. Routledge Publishing.

Chavez, N. (2024, January 11). *ADL records more than 3,200 antisemitic incidents since start of Israel-Hamas war*. CNN. https://www.cnn.com/2024/01/10/us/adl-antisemitism-reports-soar-reaj/index.html

Chism, D. (2022). *Leading your school toward equity: A practical framework for walking the talk*. ASCD.

Collins, P. (2015). Intersectionality's definition dilemmas. *Annual Review of Sociology*. https://doi.org/10.1146/annurev-soc-073014-112142.

Crenshaw, K. (1989). Demarginalizing the intersection of race and sex: A Black feminist critique of antidiscrimination doctrine, feminist theory and antiracist politics. *University of Chicago Legal Forum, 1*(8). https://chicagounbound.uchicago.edu/cgi/viewcontent.cgi?article=1052&context=uclf

Equal Employment and Opportunity Commission. *EEOC history: The law*. US EEOC. (2024). https://www.eeoc.gov/overview

Gorski, P. (2019). Avoiding racial equity detours. *Educational Leadership, 76*(7). http://www.ascd.org/publications/educational-leadership/apr19/vol76/num07/Avoiding-Racial-Equity-Detours.aspx.

hooks, b. (2009). *Belonging: A culture of place*. Routledge.

Love, B. (2023). *Punished for dreaming: How school reform harms Black children and how we heal*. St. Martin's Press.

Minow, M. (2010). *In brown's wake: Legacies of America's educational landmark*. Oxford University Press.

Reinhard, K. (2023, April 6). *CRT forward tracking project*. CRT forward releases new report on anti-CRT measures and trends – CRT Forward Tracking

Project. https://crtforward.law.ucla.edu/new-crt-forward-report-highlights-trends-in-2021-2022-anti-crt-measures/.

Rice-Boothe, M. (2023). *Leading within systems of inequity in education: A liberation guide for leaders of color*. ASCD.

Urban, W. J., & Wagoner, J. L. (2014). *American education: A history* (5th ed.). Routledge.

Wood, S. (2023, August 18). *DEI bans at colleges: What students should know* https://www.usnews.com/education/best-colleges/articles/dei-bans-at-colleges-what-students-should-know.

2

The Role of DEI Practitioners

Student outcomes should not be predictable based on race, class, or other social factors. Nevertheless, educational systems are marked by glaring inequities and forms of injustice. The field of education reflects achievement disparities, underfunded schools that lack access to resources, and disciplinary policies that result in a disproportionate number of students of color experiencing suspensions or expulsions. Advanced placement courses (AP) also demonstrate a system that often leaves racialized groups behind. As Bettina Love (2023) asserted via Education Week, our public education systems have never been *woke* because, frankly, schools are *barely awake,* as evidenced by disparities. The Office for Civil Rights (OCR) released a report in 2023 that highlighted civil rights data from the 2020 to 2021 school year. The data collection reflected over 97,000 public schools and more than 17, 000 school districts. There were different areas assessed during the global pandemic that included student enrollment, access to courses and resources, student discipline, and other climate factors. The following offers key findings from the report:

- **Access to teachers and educational staff:** Nearly 522,400 students, or 1% of the total student enrollment population, attended public schools where less than half of the teachers met state requirements for certification. The report also indicated that 77% of public schools had at least one counselor.
- **Access to advanced courses:** Black and Latino students were underrepresented in AP Computer Science, AP Science, and AP

DOI: 10.4324/9781032623542-2

Mathematics courses. Although white students only represented 48% of the total high school student enrollment, more than 50% were enrolled in AP Science and AP Math.

- **Harassment:** K-12 students reported over 42,500 allegations of harassment to school employees. Forty percent of harassment claims were on the basis of sex. Black students and children of two or more races were overrepresented in survey outcomes as being harassed or bullied as a result of their racial identities.
- **Student discipline:** Black boys were nearly two times more likely than white boys to receive an out-of-school suspension or an expulsion from a public school. Students who received one or more out-of-school-suspension missed a summation of over 2 million days of school. Black public preschool children also received out-of-school suspensions at a rate nearly twice their enrollment.

In a recent study (2024), Calvin Zimmermann examined how teachers perpetuate discipline inequities in early childhood. The study incorporated a qualitative method in behavioral and social sciences known as ethnography to examine how first-grade teachers interact with Black and white male students. Through the study, it was evident that teachers over-monitored the behaviors of Black males and anticipated disturbances. White male students were likely to evade reprimands from their teachers, while Black male students were not only singled out but given harsher consequences. The findings were similar to a research report from Yale Child Study Center (Bender, 2016) that demonstrated how preschool teachers spent more time tracking the behaviors of Black male students. Zimmermann discussed the role of unconscious biases in disciplinary responses and how institutional racism impacts young learners (DeStazio, 2024). Students who experience harm and those benefiting from an inequitable system all receive messages about belonging and justice through acts of bias.

With a critical lens, it is also important to note that numerical data does not often capture the full extent of harm that students experience in educational settings. Although metrics such as achievement data, disciplinary outcomes, and advanced placement enrollment provide useful information, they do not often convey the psychological harm, microaggressions, or identity threats students experience in schools. As practitioners, it is important for us to create opportunities for active listening. We need to understand the stories behind data to evaluate systems and the experiences of students and staff. Through the implementation of focus groups, affinity spaces, and listening tours, I have often filled in data gaps from the voices of students, families, and staff.

Educational inequities at the institutional level are reinforced through deficit ideologies. It is a way of thinking that shifts the focus from changing unjust systems to fixing individuals or communities. The unexamined ideologies (Nieto & Bode, 2008) that attribute students' academic or social challenges to perceived shortcomings are detrimental to children and widen disparities when paired with power. *This student is not capable and does not deserve access or an opportunity to be a part of the reading enrichment group.* When systemic barriers such as underfunding or institutionalized racism are ignored, students and their families are deemed as the scapegoats for poor outcomes. This blame game creates a culture that disregards a student's potential and hinders their access to opportunities.

Although all educational leaders must uphold the protection of students' civil rights, school districts have developed positions, departments, or have hired consultants to spearhead proactive measures and streamline responsive practices across systems. Chief Equity Officers, who were historically a branch of the Civil Rights Act of 1964 (Title VII), were positioned in schools as strategic, thought-leaders to address the systemic nature of educational inequalities. Although titles and initiatives may have evolved, the work to eliminate educational disparities and promote just outcomes remains the same.

The Misconceptions of DEI Practitioners

There are many misconceptions about the roles and responsibilities of DEI practitioners. In the ASCD article, *Want to Hire a DEI Officer? Here's What to Know First* (Buchanan-Rivera, 2020), I described existing fallacies of positions that are devised to advance equitable practices. One of the misconceptions is that DEI practitioners are the answer to inequitable systems, institutional racism, and discriminatory practices. Structural inequities are perpetuated through cultural norms, policies and practices, and power dynamics that surpass the influence of one person. Although a person's will and skills can empower others to act, systemic change depends on the shared responsibilities of a collective that includes teachers, superintendents, school board members, principals, counselors, educational staff, and community partnerships. One person cannot do the heavy lifting of unraveling unjust systems, and I do not advise working in isolation in efforts to protect our mental health.

Another misconception is that all DEI practitioners share identical responsibilities. School district leaders hire staff based on their community's unique needs. For instance, my first DEI role was grant funded. Although everyone was not on board with the idea of hiring a Chief Equity and Inclusion Officer, the grant writers conducted research and assessed data that supported the need for a position to streamline DEI efforts. There were glaring racial disparities and growing concerns among racialized communities regarding the lack of inclusive practices within predominantly white schools. The needs compelled a small group of district leaders to apply for a grant and advocate for a Chief Equity and Inclusion Officer. My role and responsibilities were different from some of my colleagues who were hired in other districts for damage control as a result of incidents that involved discriminatory practices. *District leaders: We are sorry this happened in our school community. We hear your outcries and have hired a person to help us be better!* The reasons behind the conception of the role often determine the job responsibilities. DEI practitioners have varied responsibilities, and their work tends to evolve based on power dynamics, policies, and the political climate.

There is also the belief that newly posted positions indicate an institution's readiness and willingness to embrace DEI initiatives. The *desire for change* and *being ready for change* are two different things. For example, the grant writers of my first DEI role desired change and robust work to support students' sense of belonging. However, people in positions of power – *school board members, superintendents, and directors* – were not ready to embrace the responsibilities or actions tied to the DEI role. My work was often undermined, board members opposed my presence, and I frequently had to defend my efforts. Although I made lifelong connections and impacted the lives of many students (who are now adulting and contact me often), I was not in an environment that was conducive to *real work* to advance equity. I lacked power and was removed from spaces where important decisions were made.

Some of my colleagues from surrounding districts were also in positions where they did not have the power to make change and were considered the "Black best friend" of their institutions. *We cannot be a racist organization, because we hired a Black DEI Officer. Look at how inclusive we are!* They left those positions within two years. Therefore, we cannot assume that a job posting for a 'VP of Culture' means that leaders and staff are ready to make cultural shifts. In *Chapter 3*, I will talk more about the concept of readiness and the questions we should ask to determine if an environment is worth our investment.

Exploring the Responsibilities of DEI Practitioners

If *'building a plane as it flies'* were a person, it would certainly be a DEI practitioner. It is an evolving role with responsibilities that change over time based on needs, opportunities, political shifts, and human interactions. What we do today may change tomorrow – *or in my experience, what was done an hour ago, may shift to an entirely different project two hours later*. We contribute to areas where we are needed and respond to new, challenging circumstances daily while engaging in human work. Although we may carry different titles and responsibilities, we have a shared purpose to create equitable systems and inclusive environments. The following areas of focus describe some of the responsibilities of DEI practitioners who may lead at a district or school-based level. This is a high-level overview that will be unpacked in upcoming chapters:

- **Cultivating a culture of mirror work:** Mirror work is an important and necessary first step for anyone who is leading a system, classroom, or school to advance equity. We all need intentional moments with ourselves to assess the shaping of our leadership identities and the experiences that drive actions and approaches. Developing a culture that is rooted in self-reflection encourages people to pause and consider their impact while working with students and families.
- **Strategic vision for equitable practices:** To advance equitable practices, we need a road map that incorporates the voices of multiple stakeholder groups. The work of creating a shared vision for equity and cohesion among educational staff is critical.
- **Disrupting deficit ideologies:** Deficit ideologies create a culture of blame within schools that sustains educational inequities. The disruption of deficit ideologies cannot occur without self-awareness and opportunities that nudge individuals to deeply interrogate their beliefs about children and how those beliefs influence their actions. DEI practitioners work to create school cultures that embrace mirror work.
- **Critically examining systems:** Being a critical examiner of systems means that we think deeply about the implications of decisions related to school operations, policies, instruction, and initiatives. We also consider the factors that perpetuate and sustain disparities. An analytical approach to problem-solving can lead to proactive strategies and informed decisions.
- **Creating conditions of belonging:** The mere presence of children within a classroom or colleagues within a workspace does not indicate belonging. People do not experience psychological safety or feel valued simply from being in a shared space with others. There is purposeful work needed to build authentic connections

and to foster caring interactions within a community. It is important for students and staff to feel as if their humanity, contributions, and presence matter. We can develop initiatives that focus on mindful communication, classroom rituals (that promote a sense of connection and safety), anti-biased education, and social-emotional learning.

- **Building knowledge and capacity:** It is important to create opportunities for professional learning where educators and staff can acquire research and a deeper understanding of DEI work. The development of a professional learning plan that aligns with institutional goals and incorporates objectives, learning outcomes, and accountability measures (ensuring that learning is debriefed, ongoing, and practiced) is a purposeful strategy for the advancement of equitable practices. Staff also need the capacity and tools to recognize and disrupt inequities in their everyday work environment.
- **Fostering collective work:** School systems consist of many departments and specialized roles that support institutional operations and the enactment of policies. This structure challenges us to foster collaboration among divisions to ensure vision alignment and shared leadership *because we are not doing this work in isolation!* We must also consider the power of partnerships, fostering trust among students, families, staff, and community members. In my experience, this could look like the development of equity-related teams, student advocacy groups, or community coalitions that create space for underrepresented voices to be heard.
- **Supporting student services:** DEI practitioners may be responsible for student services or programs. This could include the evaluations of counselors, social workers, and systems or programs (e.g., special education, multilingual departments, high ability, etc.) that support the academic needs and well-being of students. Many DEI practitioners in school districts may also commonly serve as Title IX or Title VI coordinators to enforce environments free of harassment or discrimination.
- **Developing community-based education:** Community-based education may also be a part of the job description of DEI practitioners. Given the presence of movements that mischaracterize DEI initiatives, it is helpful to provide opportunities for community stakeholders to learn about inclusive practices. As a Director of Equity and Inclusion, I developed a community coalition that empowered parents and

caregivers to create learning experiences for families (discussed in Chapter 4). Within our roles, we could consider the development of educational opportunities that invite community members to participate in learning experiences.

- **Reforming and shaping policies:** DEI practitioners should be involved in the development and enactment of district and school-based policies. If discrimination leads to unfair resource allocation and limits student access or success, policy changes may be necessary. A DEI practitioner can guide policy changes or collaborate with a team to ensure just outcomes (e.g., team consisting of superintendents, directors, parents or caregivers, teachers, administrators, etc.). Policy development involves an analysis of the problem and its potential impact (understanding who benefits or may be harmed) and the input of multiple stakeholder groups to support the decision-making process.
- **Partnering with public relations teams:** Most school corporations have people who are appointed to work on public relations (PR) and community outreach. It is important for schools to tell their story and shine a light on the ways they support the outcomes of students. Although DEI practitioners are not solely responsible for district communications, they can certainly play a role in supporting PR teams. If a school district has a commitment to equitable outcomes, community stakeholders need to see evidence of progress and visible strategies. Social media has become a great tool to market actions toward the achievement of goals. When communications are drafted for public consumption, we can request to review documents, video announcements, or newsletters with an equity lens.

This was not an all-inclusive list of job responsibilities, since every school district has unique needs, student populations, and communities. However, the areas of focus do provide a general overview of the work DEI practitioners may do within their respective environments. It is also important to reiterate that the degree of power a person holds to change systems looks different for each practitioner. Similar to my first role as a Chief Equity and Inclusion Officer, some positions are structured in ways that give practitioners no real power. I have worked with colleagues in affinity groups who were only responsible for professional learning opportunities. Their sole purpose was to contract with experts and bring in guest speakers for early release days. Responsibilities and degrees of power will vary, which is why we need to raise critical questions in interview processes about our role (*see Chapter 3*) and the readiness of a district prior to accepting positions.

Pitfalls to Avoid

While existing in a politically charged climate where DEI work is deemed as a threat, we must consider our navigation and engagement within systems. We have seen well-intentioned initiatives backfire or contribute to marginalization. There are practitioners, including myself, who have seen their own work and words used against them by political or community-based groups. DEI practitioners must actively anticipate risks and make responsible decisions. We need to consider the impact of our actions and be prepared for backlash.

Here are some pitfalls to avoid while operating in DEI roles based on personal lived experiences and debriefing sessions with colleagues. I have also invited fellow DEI practitioners to share their insights as well. You cannot always avoid 'the messy,' but you can potentially circumvent missteps to sustain your work:

1 **Do not make the assumption that everyone, including those who hired you, understands the nuances of achieving educational equity**. We may be situated in schools or divisions where people have never publicly talked about race, bias, or inclusive practices. Despite making it through several interview rounds and securing a job, our purpose, strengths, and approach to advance equity may still be questioned or challenged. Therefore, it is important to listen and assess people's knowledge, will, skills, and capacity to advance equity. We cannot assume that everyone shares the same baseline knowledge for DEI work.

2 **Consider the pace of change.** Although children deserve to be in joyful, human-centered spaces, we know that the creation of just conditions takes time and does not happen through quick-fix solutions or unrealistic demands. Change requires a thoughtful process and an analysis of impact. For example, I worked in a district that was exploring the idea of systematically changing grading practices in secondary education. As a Director of Equity of Inclusion, I researched equitable grading practices and found many articles for my team's exploration. District leaders used those articles and learned from professional development experiences to make decisions about grading practices that did not initially involve teachers, parents, or my oversight. The

pressure to overhaul an old grading system led to rapid decision-making that was not vetted by multiple stakeholders. It did not take long to see complaints rolling in from the community as some students dropped letter grades, and teachers were concerned. Although accelerated change is desirable, the push for swift results can lead to missteps, confusion, and the omission of valuable perspectives if the approach lacks intentionality. We cannot "burn it all down" if we only have a concept of a plan and lack an understanding of people's needs or knowledge of how to rebuild systems. It is humane to stop harm when it occurs, yet we must be strategic in our approach and consider the sustainability of just practices.

3 **Make sure tasks align with goals that work toward equitable outcomes.** Responsibilities should reflect efforts to support achievement and positive school experiences for students. When I accepted my first DEI role, I spent a lot of time working with students and organizing professional learning experiences (anti-racism training and anti-biased education), yet I was detached from curricular and instructional teams to impact achievement outcomes. Since I was hired to address achievement disparities, my work should have centered on culturally responsive instruction. It is important to look at the roles and responsibilities of your job description to determine your potential impact and how the role will be leveraged in an organization. We should not be afraid to talk to supervisors if our job description evolves into work that is misaligned with goals.

4 **Do not embrace the role of the "race relations whisperer."** People of color in DEI positions are frequently asked to address racial issues. For example, if a Black parent expressed a concern via email, some principals (who did not identify as Black) would immediately contact me instead of directly engaging with the parent to understand their perspective. While DEI practitioners may be equipped to address school or district-level issues, colleagues should not be conditioned to opt out of conversations about race. For my colleagues of color, we cannot build capacity or focus on institutional goals if we are constantly called to be the spokesperson for racial disparities or incidents. We should thoughtfully decide when to lead or give guidance. Anyone who supports students should feel compelled to work with their parents or caregivers. We may share resources, insights, and guidance, but should not help people sidestep conversations about race.

Here are some additional pitfalls to avoid from other current and former practitioners from public school districts:

- *Thinking that you can make significant change without the district leadership truly being invested in the work is a definite pitfall. (Terri, former DEI practitioner from Indiana)*
- *Ensure that school-based equity teams understand their roles and meet consistently. (Patricia Payne, Director of the IPS Office of Strategic Educational Excellence from Indiana)*
- *Watch out for the PR person in the district spinning your work. Make sure whatever is publicized captures your intentions and purpose. (Terri, former DEI practitioner from Indiana)*
- *You also cannot wait until everyone cares to start doing the work. (Ayva Thomas, Executive Director of Organizational Change and Student Advancement and Ranna Harb, Organizational Change and Student Advancement Specialist from Washington)*

Naming the Risks

Any work that requires truth-telling and the disruption of the status quo will come with risks. People often fear what they do not understand. Fear, coupled with harmful ideologies or prejudices, can also drive people to acts of dehumanization. We may experience harm in the form of resistance, threats, petitions, and public defamation. One of the first petitions against my role involved a principal's decision to focus on celebrations of learning, rather than the 'holidays,' which was a code word for Christmas. She supported winter-themed celebrations yet proposed for them to occur following the break to take the emphasis off of one holiday. There were many students who did not celebrate Christmas, and she was actively trying not to exclude them.

We discussed her options and the potential consequences of her decisions. I shared how I would support her efforts to focus on winter-themed celebrations and encouraged the acknowledgement of multiple holiday observances as an educational opportunity for students – *offering guidance and not dictating how a principal should operate a building*. After her decision was made to focus on winter celebrations, a petition soon emerged within the community to reinstate traditional Christmas parties. The petition argued that every student should have the opportunity to watch Polar Express, wrap gifts for their parents, and enjoy sweet treats. In other words, the petition advocated for all students to conform to the values and traditions of the protestors. It also conveyed that the principal's decision to focus on winter-themed celebrations was directly related to the hiring of my role. In our efforts to foster inclusive spaces, we might encounter audacious behaviors, opposition, or conduct that disregards people's humanity.

DEI work is not about unifying people to function and exist in inequitable environments. It is about the construction of a new foundation with conditions that generate a sense of belonging. Some students might have enjoyed wrapping presents for their parents during class, but others could have experienced distress from the activity (e.g., students who have experienced the loss of a parent, foster care systems, etc.). Not every holiday-themed movie conveys the best messaging for human development, either. Frankly, my child and I both find Polar Express unsettling and creepy during certain points of the movie. Unfortunately, we exist in a world where many people uphold assimilationist values and expect for others to conform to their ways of being. There are people who believe that some communities are not worthy of grace, resources (e.g., SNAP benefits, health insurance, free lunch programs, etc.), or recognition. As DEI practitioners, we are challenged to work through the varying belief systems that exist within a school community and serve as barriers to progress.

It is hard to fathom the backlash one could receive for doing their job. I have talked to many DEI practitioners who have felt a wave of punishment for making visible progress toward equitable outcomes. When working in areas or with people who uphold white supremacy culture or dehumanizing beliefs, it can be difficult to combat racist ideologies and movements that preach the horrors of DEI. Practitioners of color may face greater challenges or risks when leading authentically or confronting institutional racism in these communities.

My first DEI role was positioned in a suburban, predominantly white school district. Although I wanted to be immersed in more curricular systems, I must give myself credit for the learning experiences I initiated and their impact on teachers. A right-wing column published an article discussing a teacher's instructional lesson on wage gaps from my school district. The lesson caught the attention of a parent, who reported the teacher to various media outlets. He believed the lesson was a form of indoctrination despite its connection to academic standards. The article claimed that the high school was *going woke* as a result of my role and presence in the district. This led to online threats, harassment, and the phone call from a friend (shared in Introduction) telling me to save myself.

I do not share these contextual experiences to shy anyone away from DEI practitioner roles. Many fellow DEI practitioners who are a part of my community have done incredible work for students, teachers, and families. We are proud of our efforts, courageousness, and the lives that have been changed through our advocacy. However, I would be negligent if I were dismissive of the risks of our work while existing in an anti-DEI climate. We know that many DEI departments across the country are being dismantled

(Bennett & Norris, 2024), teaching contracts are being terminated, and roadblocks constantly emerge as a result of anti-DEI policies. The emotional battle wounds are real, which requires a discussion about wellness, self-care, and the development of support systems (see Chapter 7).

Chapter Highlights

1. Educational systems are marked with blatant disparities across race and class that are connected to systemic racism and poverty within society. DEI practitioners are called to engage educational leaders, teachers, community members, and students in collective work to transform schools into anti-discriminatory spaces that center justice and humanizing approaches.
2. Addressing systemic inequities within schools requires collective responsibility; it cannot rest solely on DEI practitioners. All leaders, educators, and staff members should commit to fostering environments where students can thrive and achieve success. Although the elimination of inequities is a shared obligation, DEI practitioners can play a pivotal role in organizing, championing, and assessing these initiatives.
3. While each DEI position comes with its own set of responsibilities, all share the objective of fostering equitable practices and inclusive environments. If certain tasks seem disconnected from these aims or appear merely performative – *meaning they look positive outwardly but fail to deliver real justice or support within the institution* – it's crucial to advocate for a reassessment of duties.
4. There are many pitfalls and risks that exist in the field of DEI work. We need to consider proactive methods, the pacing of initiatives, and how we engage with others.

Mirror Work

1. When you review the responsibilities and common themes of DEI practitioner roles, what stands out as a personal strength? Which areas require more growth and support?
2. What excites you or holds you back as you consider leading systems for equity?
3. What do you consider when critically evaluating systems? See Figure 2.1.

Critical Questions for Equitable Systems for Support
Critical Questions for Curriculum
1. Are the lessons, activities, assessments, and course materials accessible to all students? 2. How do the lessons align with standards and prepare students for summative assessments? 3. How do course materials benefit all students (e.g., multilingual learners, racialized communities, students with disabilities, etc.)? 4. How do the lessons, content, or activities honor the histories, identities, or lived experiences of students? 5. Which voices or stories are centered in the unit, lesson, or curriculum? Are there biases or misrepresentations of communities presented within course materials? 6. Do the lessons or units offer students a space to process the world around them? 7. How does the curriculum support human development?
Critical Questions for Policy Work:
1. Who is involved in policy development? 2. How is the policy supported by research? (e.g., outcomes from the enactment of policies have been studied) 3. How do we measure the impact of policies? 4. How does the policy consider the identities and lived experiences of the people it impacts?
Critical Questions for School Operations:
1. How do school procedures impact the well-being of students? 2. Are the workloads and expectations consistent with the vision and goals of the school or district? 3. How do expectations and job responsibilities impact the well-being of staff? 4. Does initiative overload exist? How do you know?
Critical Questions about Pedagogy:
1. How do we define a best practice and by whose standard? 2. When we assert that a pedagogical approach is a best practice, who is it 'best' for? 3. What do we look for as evidence of culturally responsive teaching?
Critical Questions about Student Discipline:
1. What are our beliefs about student discipline? 2. What is our approach for supporting the behavioral and emotional needs of students? 3. What research supports our discipline policies, approaches, and practices? 4. How do our discipline policies or practices foster partnerships with parents or caregivers? 5. How are our disciplinary practices trauma-informed?

Figure 2.1 Critical questions for equitable systems.

References

Bender, M. (2016, October 4). Yale study tests implicit bias of preschool teachers. Yale News. https://yaledailynews.com/articles/yale-study-tests-implicit-bias-of-preschool-teachers

Bennett, G., & Norris, C. (2024, August 27). *How some companies are scaling back DEI initiatives after conservative backlash*. PBS. https://www.pbs.org/newshour/show/how-some-companies-are-scaling-back-dei-initiatives-after-conservative-backlash

Buchanan-Rivera, E. (2020, July 29). *Want to hire a DEI officer: Here's what to know first*. ASCD. https://www.ascd.org/blogs/want-to-hire-a-diversity-equity-inclusion-officer-heres-what-to-know-first

DeStazio, T. (2024, February 9). *"I'm watching you" behavior produces racial disparities in school discipline*. Notre Dame News. https://news.nd.edu/news/im-watching-you-behavior-produces-racial-disparities-in-school-discipline/

Love, B. (2023, August 15). *No, public education isn't too woke. It's barely even awake (opinion)*. Education Week.

Nieto, S., & Bode, P. (2008). *Affirming diversity: The sociopolitical context of multicultural education, 5/e*. Pearson.

Zimmermann, C. R. (2024). Looking for trouble: How Teachers' racialized practices perpetuate discipline inequities in early childhood. *Sociology of Education, 0*(0). https://doi.org/10.1177/00380407241228581

3

Finding the Right Institution to Do the Work

Although the advancement of educational equity is a critical objective, it is also human work and arguably, one of the most complex group assignments. With any group project, you encounter a myriad of belief systems, motives, and dispositions. There are people who serve as visionaries and generate ideas, while others are more task-oriented and focus on process execution. Some team members offer moral support and encouragement, while other colleagues contribute specialized skills. There are staff members who dominate discussions, adding little to no value, who love to hear themselves talk. Unfortunately, working partnerships may also include saboteurs or naysayers who are counterproductive and act to derail progress.

The success of DEI initiatives depends on organizational group dynamics and the way individuals exercise their power within the workplace. Understanding individuals' beliefs and governance structures are essential for assessing whether a school community's environment is conducive to DEI work. Too often, DEI practitioners walk into an educational setting with a spirit of optimism, only to discover a combative working environment. It is difficult to lead change within a school community if people on the inside and outside of an institution are working together to undermine DEI efforts. Therefore, I highly encourage all DEI practitioners to find an institution with leaders who *have the will* to protect and promote efforts toward equitable outcomes. No institution led by humans will ever be perfect, yet it makes a world of difference to know that you will not be alone on the frontlines of injustice. You are worthy of a group project where most people understand the assignment.

DOI: 10.4324/9781032623542-3

Considering a DEI Role

There are several factors to consider before accepting a job offer. It's important to ask about work expectations, salary, benefits, work-life balance, and opportunities for growth. We should do our homework and thoroughly research organizations of interest. Although life can present circumstances that force us to go against our better judgment (i.e., taking a job that is not a top choice, yet needed for survival, insurance, etc.), it is ideal to find an environment that suits our gifts and aligns with our beliefs about justice. We should learn about the function, mission, and leadership of an organization before stepping into a role.

For DEI practitioners, it is essential to assess an organization's dedication to the advancement of educational equity. Key principles of commitment encompass the placement of the DEI role within organizational leadership structures, allocation of resources for equity-driven initiatives, and the formulation of strategic objectives. It is also important to assess policies and the political climate within a school community. Here are some other considerations for your homework while exploring DEI-related job opportunities in educational contexts:

- **Study school data:** Demographic, academic, and behavioral (e.g., attendance and discipline) data are indicators of potential needs and strategies for implementation. Drill down into the disparities within data and review how the language or actions within strategic plans align with the inequities you have identified.
- **Political climate:** Anti-DEI legislation is a significant obstacle for school districts. Between curricular censorship codified into laws and well-funded political groups (e.g., local and national) taking on the role of enforcers, a DEI practitioner should consider the geographical location of their work. It is important to determine if a district or school environment will be conducive to policy work and systemic changes that honor the humanity of all students. When researching school districts, type the name of the school or organization with accompanying terms such as racism, indoctrination, DEI, book bans, or gender ideology to see what surfaces—*I do this often when deciding where I would like to consult too.* If we are in positions that force us to ban books or create discriminatory policies, it will be hard to sell our role as a champion of DEI work when people see us and our complicitness as a part of the problem.
- **Office for Civil Rights:** The OCR has historically published a list of elementary, secondary, and post-secondary institutions that are

under investigation for discrimination (see references for link). It would be wise to know if you are stepping into a ring of fire, and to consider your potential involvement with families, students, attorneys, and media. (*Note that the function of the OCR and its definitions of discrimination will continue to change with guidance from new administrations.*)

- **Anti-discrimination and harassment policies:** There are many policies within district and school handbooks that could be reviewed through a lens of equity. For a preliminary assessment, it would be beneficial to review the language and communities described in policies regarding harassment and discrimination. Note the communities that are included in protective measures and how a district intends to respond to allegations of discrimination.
- **Evolution of position:** It is important to know the origin story of a DEI position and whether it is sustainable. Investigate the funding sources for the position, examining how it was developed (if such information is available).
- **Platforms of school board members:** School board members are responsible for the evaluations of superintendents, which means that members with a political agenda could influence the decisions of educational leaders and eliminate structures that promote DEI work (e.g., terminating contracts for consultants, professional development, and DEI-related positions). Research the platforms of board members and understand the reasons that prompted them to run for their position. For instance, I resided in a community that had a slate of conservative candidates who ran with the platform of saving schools, protecting children, and restoring academic excellence- *coded language for 'remove all things DEI'*. After the slate of candidates won, they forced out the district's first Black superintendent and eliminated the contract of the Chief Equity and Inclusion Officer.
- **Visibility of mission:** Note if the district's beliefs about DEI are visible. Is there a mission related to DEI work? How does the mission on the district's website or publications translate to the work happening in schools across the district? Some school websites might avoid using equity terminology to safeguard their funding as a result of anti-DEI policies. However, you should look for wording that highlights belonging, access, and underscores the value of respecting every student and member within the school community. If the position is new and there is no evidence or promotion of DEI initiatives, it may signal the need for foundational equity work.

Interviewing for a DEI Practitioner Role

When preparing for an interview related to a DEI role, we need to consider our ability to lead collective efforts among people with varying belief systems. How do we navigate a group project that is designed to transform systems? We may receive questions about community engagement, approaches to conflict, and how we inspire change. In my interview experiences, I recalled being asked questions about culturally responsive pedagogy and the root causes of racial disparities in schools. I was also tasked to develop a strategic plan and goals based on my own data analysis of inequities within a school district. No matter the question, it is helpful to have responses grounded in research and contextual experiences. When talking about instructional practices, draw from your experiences with school-based teams, students, and families. Paint a clear picture of your leadership in action, rather than a projection of platitudes.

Most interview processes also leave room for questions from candidates. This is a prime opportunity to learn more about an organization's commitment to equity. If the DEI position is the 'first' for a school district, you may want to learn about its evolution and the reasons behind the new role, as previously discussed. On the other hand, if you are the third or fourth person to potentially accept a DEI role after multiple resignations, you may want to know more about working conditions and why the position is symbolic of a revolving door. Here are some additional interview questions to help you consider the right environments for DEI work:

1. **Structure:** What is the current structure of DEI work? Are there district-level or school-based teams? Who do I supervise? Is there a DEI department? Who is my direct report?
2. **Time allotment:** If I could create a pie chart of roles and responsibilities (e.g., curriculum, instruction, public relations, etc.), where would you envision most of my time being spent based on how the position is structured?
3. **Collaboration:** Based on the organizational flow chart, who will I primarily collaborate with to execute strategies from the strategic plan?
4. **Positioning:** Most school districts have a cabinet or an executive team that makes impactful decisions. Will I be a part of an executive team or hold a cabinet position? Will I be in spaces where decisions are made or far removed?
5. **Budget:** What is the annual budget for my role? Who approves DEI-related expenses? If the position is grant-funded, what funding will be used to sustain the position? (Note: There will be a time when language does not have to be altered to receive the funding that is needed.)

6 **Protection:** How will I be protected from backlash for doing my job? Who will provide support or protection should petitions arise in opposition to my initiatives? How does the organization support the mental well-being of employees?
7 **Glows and grows:** What strategies have been proven effective from the strategic plan to advance equity? What are some areas of growth based on the implementation of strategies? Why do you think those strategies were ineffective?

If I asked some of these questions prior to accepting my first DEI position, I may have looked for other opportunities. I should have strayed away from a grant-funded position that lacked a department and came with an expiration date. There were no systems or people to support my efforts, which forced me to build and advocate for my own coalitions. I was initially confident that leaders would find ways to renew my contract with other funding sources. However, human interactions with school board members made that confidence dwindle and encouraged me to find other opportunities long before the end of the grant cycle.

It is also worthy to note that the responses you receive from interview questions may not align with the actions that are practiced. Many people involved in my first interview process discussed the spirit of teamwork, but I did not feel a sense of unity when community members attacked DEI efforts and my character. I was also informed that equity work was a shared vision throughout the school district, but the lack of coherence among schools demonstrated that efforts were not widely practiced, understood, or embraced. No matter what you hear and process, sometimes you must trust your instincts. The following section will further examine the factors that inform our intuition when selecting an institution to lead DEI work.

Red Flags

True story. A couple of years after having my first child, my husband and I were house hunting. We anticipated growing our family and looked for a bigger space. Our realtor encouraged us to visit a single-family home that checked most of our boxes. Upon entering the residence, we noted the open floor plan and the thoughtful architectural design. The color schemes on the first level appeared to be warm and inviting. When we ventured upstairs, we noted that the rooms were orderly yet antiquated. There were vintage furnishings and styles that contradicted the contemporary look on the first floor. It felt as though we had traveled back to another era. We perused the bedrooms and noticed some interesting decor. There were figurines of monkeys with cymbals and an abundance of ventriloquist dolls. Suddenly, the well-polished home with an initial feeling of warmth had an aura of eeriness. As we explored the basement, we found dozens of dilapidated, Annabelle-looking dolls shoved into a storage closet. This was the final straw, and it was time to look for a new house.

Many of us have experienced situations that have exposed red flags. We hear comments or see things around us that serve as warning signs of danger. Red flags are an internal alarm that signify the need to pause and reflect, or to regroup and move in a new direction. There are red flags that cause us to pivot from relationships or new opportunities, like buying a home! When we are presented with areas of caution, we must consider the risks and decide if we have the will to proceed.

There are many educational institutions that signal red flags as related to DEI work. Personally, I will not consider a DEI role if several Black people resigned from the same position. The resignations convey a message about belonging that I do not want to experience. If district leaders elevate the importance of diversity and lack multiple racial perspectives on their leadership teams, that is also a red flag. Similar to my house-hunting experience, candidates of DEI positions must examine the aspects of an institution that appear or feel unsettling. We need to identify risks and determine if we have the capacity to proceed.

The following conveys additional red flags that may emerge during an interview process or through self-research. Certain red flags can become apparent based on the responses from interview questions. Remember, a red flag does not mean that we must turn down an opportunity. However, we need to consider dealbreakers and think about the areas that could change with thoughtful feedback. We must discern the difference between intuition and fear of embracing a new challenge. Here are some circumstances that have the potential to hinder the progress of a DEI practitioner's role.

- **No budget for DEI initiatives or work.** This indicates a lack of investment in the resources and educational experiences needed to change systems and outcomes for students. If you want to make cultural shifts, you will need resources to support your efforts, which requires an adequate amount of funding.
- **Position focuses more on the curation of professional development, community engagement opportunities, or student clubs.** Although many of us may enjoy social experiences and fellowship, we are not hired to be a party planner within an institution. If our roles focus on event planning for educational and cultural experiences, we probably won't be involved in efforts that analyze student data or outcomes. International festivals and hour-long workshops are not the remedy to disparities. Learning

opportunities are enriching and needed (yes, please plan all the things), but we also need time to assess conditions for learning and engage in strategic work.

- **You are the DEI department.** We need a team of highly trained people to support, coach, and promote equitable practices. Do not accept a role where you are the lone ranger. A school district should provide names of teams, departments, or individuals who will work within your division to collaborate and foster collective efforts.
- **It is a grant-funded position.** There are amazing grants that will fund the development of innovative positions. These grants will likely have strict accountability measures and may assess areas of interest that do not align with your district's strategic plan (especially if an organization wants to utilize data for a particular motive). You will be bound to grant *and* district-level expectations. Additionally, the funding comes with a short shelf life. In other words, after the grant cycle, the DEI position may not be absorbed into district budgets and could be eliminated. If considering a grant-funded position, ask about the longevity of the role after the grant funds are no longer available.
- **Your position is housed under the Human Resources (HR) department.** Support HR work, yet do not immerse yourself in the responsibilities of an HR department. If you find yourself in this division, you are bound to be in a constant state of reactionary work and will barely be involved in pedagogical shifts. My first DEI role was housed in HR. The department was isolating and did not connect to the work I was doing with teachers and staff. Therefore, I advocated to be a part of the Teaching and Learning division, where I gained a better pulse of student data, programs, and curriculum.

Some of you may have reviewed the red flags and said, *What if these red flags are evident in my current workplace?* Great question. There's no need to panic, yet there may be a need for courageous conversations. If a budget does not exist, we can suggest the importance of funding to support the improvement of systems and propose a list of needed items with costs. If positioned in an HR department, create a compelling case for switching to a division that will prioritize student-centered work. In both of my roles, I served as a cabinet member, but I was not a part of the executive leadership teams that consisted of the superintendent, assistant superintendent(s), and HR director(s). Therefore, I personally requested to have meetings with superintendents directly, and over time, I was invited into those executive spaces after building rapport with leaders. Sometimes you have to advocate for yourself to shift the red flag to a green light.

If you are questioning your position while working in a space with red flags, I would also encourage you to reflect on your impact. Do you feel like your work is making a difference in the eyes of children? Are you seeing any signs of momentum or a difference in conversations about DEI work since your hiring? How would you describe your mental health and overall well-being in the workplace? Do you have people in positions of power who are an unapologetic force of support for you? Remember, the institution was likely on fire before our arrival, and the pacing of initiatives and desired outcomes will look different in every school or district. Do not underestimate the seeds you have planted. The work I completed in most places allowed the next person to run. We all serve a purpose.

Know Your Worth

DEI practitioner roles are challenging because the positions stand for everything our world has not been. The gifts you bring into a school corporation will be invaluable. Therefore, I encourage you to consider your worth, the scope of work, and the benefits a district should offer. Compensation is important. The work of fostering cultural shifts to generate equitable outcomes is a heavy lift and should be compensated with a reasonable salary or stipend (e.g., such as equity coaches who are teachers that work outside of their contractual hours) that recognizes the value of this labor.

Also, consider institutions that are conducive to DEI work with leadership teams who will work in tandem with you. We deserve support. We deserve a team. We deserve a space where shared power exists. We deserve to be at the table making decisions. Although teams may not always agree, we deserve a community of believers who have the will to do what is best for all children. I appreciate spaces where I can go in rounds with colleagues about a particular issue of disagreement and walk out of that discussion with a feeling of mutual respect. It is possible to be in a space with imperfect people who are willing to show up for humanity. Know your worth and never stop advocating for yourself.

Chapter Highlights

1 Do your homework. Make sure to thoroughly research and assess a school district's commitment to educational justice. Consider factors including a school district's geographical location, school board members' platforms, and local news stories to inform you of needs or potential fires.

2 In an interview process, make sure to ask about the evolution and sustainability of the DEI practitioner role. *How was the role funded? Why does it exist?* Know how your role is structured within an organizational flow chart. Strive to understand the political landscape of the school district and how it will impact your work.
3 Trust your intuition if red flags emerge. If the position feels performative or you sense a lack of support systems, you may want to save yourself from potential harm. Also, remember that red flags can also be addressed through critical conversations (see Chapter 5). If something feels off, communicate what you need and assess the responses. If your advocacy is disregarded and the environment feels hostile, we have our answer regarding whether we can do meaningful DEI work.

Mirror Work

1 What are you looking for within an institution that values DEI work? What are your dealbreakers? Unpack your own beliefs as you navigate interview processes.
2 What additional questions need to be explored in order for you to commit to a DEI practitioner role within school or school district?

Resources

Office for Civil Rights. *Pending Cases Currently Under Investigation at Elementary-Secondary and Post-Secondary Schools.* https://ocrcas.ed.gov/open-investigations?field_ois_state=653&field_ois_discrimination_statute=All&field_ois_type_of_discrimination=All&items_per_page=20&field_ois_institution=&field_ois_institution_type=All&field_open_investigation_date_1=&field_open_investigation_date_2=&field_open_investigation_date=&field_open_investigation_date_3=

4

Building Capacity for DEI Work

Addressing inequities within educational systems requires a distribution of power and collaboration among multiple school divisions, departments, and stakeholder groups to remove institutional barriers. It is transformative to have a structure of individuals or teams who are leveraged to accelerate cultural shifts, streamline communication, and revitalize equity commitments while upholding accountability systems. For DEI practitioners, building capacity may involve advocacy for positions or cadres that serve as a nucleus for bolstering proficiency and efforts toward equitable practices.

Equity teams, specialists, coalitions, and student advocacy groups are components of school communities that drive purposeful DEI work. Specialist roles and equity teams can be capacity-building tools that address student achievement, policy issues, malpractices, or the redistribution of resources within a school district. Community coalitions and student advocacy groups can also be developed as an arm of support to guide district leadership and promote inclusive school cultures. These individuals or groups can work closely with DEI practitioners to help leadership teams understand the impact of district initiatives, areas of growth, and needs within a school community.

School-Based Equity Teams

Building leadership capacity within schools is instrumental for the advancement of justice-centered work. Although school districts have overarching goals to achieve positive outcomes for students, each school has its own

DOI: 10.4324/9781032623542-4

unique population with accompanying measures and plans for improvement. Equity teams are school-based or district-level groups that are designed to problem-solve complex issues and advance goals with an anti-bias and anti-racist lens. School-based equity teams may consist of principals, teachers, counselors, and designated educational staff who meet regularly to address the inequalities within systems. Participants collaborate to identify institutional practices that do not adequately serve all students, and work to cultivate affirming and responsive school environments. School-based equity teams are designed to support students, families, and staff while examining and responding to curricular, social, and political issues within the workspace.

Equity teams within schools may be referenced as other names across districts, especially in light of ongoing anti-DEI legislation that requests the erasure of equity terminology. For example, several years ago I worked with a high school that referred to their working group as the Justice League. It was the team's way of making the group sound more intriguing with a Marvel movie vibe. No matter the name, school-based equity teams should work in partnership with principals to build skills, knowledge, and capacity among staff for culturally sustaining and inclusive practices. Ideally, equity teams should report to district-level DEI practitioners who can maintain a pulse of progress across all schools.

Equity teams invite participation from individuals who are highly motivated to promote institutional change. However, it is important to note that school-based equity teams do not bear the sole responsibility of implementing strategies toward goals and school improvement. Every member of a school district should operate with the expectation of meeting the social and academic needs of students. Every teacher should feel compelled to see children as fully human. Members of equity teams can build momentum and influence cultural shifts that yield to the prioritization of culturally relevant pedagogies and responsive practices within schools. Here are other actions or areas of focus implemented by school-based equity teams:

1. **Fostering mirror work:** School-based equity teams can help to create a culture of reflective practitioners where teachers and staff unpack their contributions to just conditions. School cultures that prioritize equity consist of teachers and educational staff who are not afraid to shine a light on themselves and interrogate the ideologies, practices, or initiatives that stifle progress toward equitable outcomes.
2. **Eliminating of disparities:** School-based equity teams focus on the elimination of disparities that impact student wellness and achievement. This may include an examination of disciplinary,

academic, or school climate data. Team members collaborate to address the root cause of inequities and work to seek solutions.

3 **Soliciting feedback and amplifying diverse perspectives:** School-based equity teams can assess how teachers, staff, and students feel about initiatives, programs, policies, curriculum, grading practices, and use feedback as a catalyst for change. For example, I participated in an elementary school's equity team meeting where members focused on the correlation between gentle entry procedures and disciplinary referrals. The team suggested a structure that would mandate social-emotional learning lessons during the first hour of instruction. Many team members wrestled with this idea and questioned if colleagues found the adopted SEL curriculum useful. The team also wanted a pulse of how teachers were implementing SEL instruction in classrooms. Through a productive discussion, the equity team members decided to assess the fidelity of schoolwide SEL initiatives prior to a systemic change.

4 **Offering ongoing professional learning opportunities:** School-based equity teams can have a positive influence on professional learning, especially when led by fellow teachers. When teachers lead with authenticity and model practices from firsthand experiences, it can make learning meaningful and accessible for colleagues (Berg, 2022). Solidarity among teachers is a transformative tool that motivates collaboration, risk-taking, and professional growth. One teacher-led experience I particularly enjoyed from an equity team was a session that focused on anti-bias education. The teacher actively demonstrated her personal work of deconstructing internalized whiteness and courageously shared her pedagogical missteps to encourage others to lean into mirror work. It was a humbling experience where she offered strategies and a space for colleagues in a predominantly white setting to engage in self-awareness. (Note: *The teacher also processed her plan with me to ensure a culturally responsive and collaborative session.*)

5 **Creating an identity-affirming school culture:** All students, families, and school staff deserve an educational environment where they can be their authentic selves. Equity teams can disrupt traditions or address practices that cause psychological harm. For example, I worked alongside an instructional coach who played an active role on her elementary school's equity team. She promoted various religious and cultural events, curated book lists for teachers (complete with inclusion-focused lesson plans), created read-aloud recordings for students to use at home, and developed reflective

questions for staff. All of those efforts were aimed at supporting the school's commitment to building an inclusive community.

6 **Identifying systems or initiatives that are a source of marginalization:** Teachers have the advantage of acquiring knowledge of students' lived experiences within school settings. Through the perspectives of students and their families, school-based equity teams can identify areas of focus that yield to deliberate actions. Teams should recognize systemic structures that lead to marginalization and feel empowered to discuss solutions to inequities among members and school leaders. For instance, I collaborated with equity teams who discovered that school events often coincided with religious observances of students and faculty. In response, these school-based equity teams collaborated across buildings to establish a comprehensive religious calendar and provided professional learning opportunities focused on religious diversity.
7 **Making equity efforts visible:** School-based equity teams can amplify efforts toward goals and an inclusive culture through publications (e.g., newsletters, brochures, flyers, etc.), social media accounts that focus on DEI work, and community partnerships.
8 **Building coalitions with families, particularly of marginalized student populations:** School-based equity teams can include students as well as families. There are school leaders who may incorporate community members in their equity teams or collaborate with parent-teacher associations. During my principalship, the school district where I worked adopted equity leadership models from the book, *Courageous Conversations About Race* (Singleton & Linton, 2006). Our equity teams developed parent-caregiver groups (PASS) that specifically invited families from minoritized groups to elevate their voice toward student achievement efforts.
9 **Normalizing conversations about educational justice:** Equity teams can model, foster, and normalize a common language for justice. When critical conversations about race, mental health, and other aspects of humanity are normalized, it creates a school culture where equity-minded people feel safe and empowered to express themselves. Appendix A demonstrates a 'Common Language' document I developed to normalize equity literacy among school-based teams. I recognize that we exist in times where it is a risk to define equity terminology. Yet, we must remember that a shared vision for equity cannot exist if coherence lacks. Equity teams can normalize topics that are often stigmatized.

Building a School-Based Equity Team

Principals should establish a clear purpose for school-based equity teams before recruiting members, ensuring everyone understands the group's objectives. Teachers and school staff members need to understand the commitments of an equity team and how they will invest their time. As DEI practitioners, we can work closely with school leaders to ensure an alignment between the purpose of an equity team and district goals. The following list articulates key considerations for principals who desire to build a school-based equity team:

1 Representation of members
2 Approach for recruitment
3 Accountability systems
4 Time and compensation

Representation

Consider the voices that should represent a school community through the work of an equity team. To address complex issues effectively, it is important to consider each member's strengths, cultural perspectives, and expertise. Teams should include a representation of different faculty and staff members, including administrators, teachers, counselors and/or social workers, and instructional coaches. Members should also reflect diversity across race, ability, gender, and identities to ensure a wide range of perspectives. The diversity within a school community should be represented in an equity team. A diverse representation of members compels participants to see complex issues through different lenses. Figure 4.1 lists potential staff who should be considered for a school-based equity team.

Potential Participants for School-Based Equity Teams
1. Principal (Requirement) 2. Assistant principal 3. Dean 4. Teacher representatives from each grade level and department or program (e.g., special education, multilingual education, high ability, dual language, etc.) 5. School counselor 6. School-based social worker 7. School psychologist 8. Instructional coach or interventionist 9. Student representative 10. Parent or caregiver representative

Figure 4.1 Potential participants for school-based-equity teams.

Based on demographics and the geographical location of a school district, it may be challenging to achieve a collective that reflects the racial and cultural diversity of its community. For schools in this scenario, it may be helpful for principals to connect with community-based organizations or consultants who are mission-aligned. Students or families could also be a consideration for involvement, depending on the structure of the equity team and topics for discussion. If the team is structured to discuss specific student data or situations that may violate privacy rights, the incorporation of external stakeholders may not be appropriate in efforts to protect students.

Approach for recruitment of equity team members

School leaders must determine a recruitment approach that will foster intentionality and progress toward goals. It is beneficial to have people who are committed to mirror work and walk in their beliefs about justice. One strategy for recruitment is an 'opt-in approach' where a principal elicits interest and people volunteer to join a team. The benefit of this method is that a school leader gains a group of highly motivated individuals who desire to lead and drive equitable changes. However, a drawback of the 'opt-in approach' is that only a few people may participate (ex. only 2 people show interest), limiting perspectives from different school roles, programs, or cultural backgrounds.

Another approach is an appointment process. Principals can appoint specific staff members who represent different areas of interest. Perhaps, a principal determines that each grade level or department has a representative on the equity team and selects staff from other divisions (e.g., school counseling, special education, multilingual departments, etc.) to participate. This approach may ensure that the collective can speak to the needs of all students within a school community. However, the downside of this approach is that a school leader risks appointing someone who has not done internal work to understand the team's purpose or feels resentment toward the assignment. I have visited school-based equity cadres where members were disgruntled and openly shared that they never asked to join a team. *I don't know how I was selected for this team. There are many things I could be doing with my time right now.*

When people are resentful of mandates or are appointed with the wrong motives, resistance can emerge and sabotage progress as well as the mission of an equity team. For example, when I resigned from my first DEI role, several staff known as equity coaches reached out to discuss the hardships of rebuilding their teams. There were teachers who stepped down from equity teams following my resignation, which forced school leaders to determine their own approach for recruitment. Equity coaches shared that some teachers were recruited and placed on teams to 'balance' the perspectives within the group dynamic. Therefore, it was not surprising to see my successor's emails to equity teams, broadcasted on social media through parental groups to generate division and outrage. When people do not want to be a part of something or have a hidden agenda, they will undermine efforts and conspire against you—*like sharing your internal, work-related e-mails to community members or right-wing groups.*

Another recruitment method could be the development of an application process (see Appendix B). The scenario regarding the public broadcasting of internal school information demonstrates the importance of vetting team members or ensuring that individuals are mission-focused. District-level DEI practitioners could consider the development of an application for school leaders' recruitment process. The application could include questions pertaining to interests, beliefs about justice, and leadership experiences. If a school district lacks a DEI district administrator, the application process could potentially be developed by a principal in partnership with a DEI consultant. An application should draw out beliefs and declarations (ex. *Here's how I practice antiracism in schools…*) that align with the mission of an equity team. Like any application process, a review team, time, and criteria are needed to make determinations of candidates. For this reason, an application process may not be feasible for some school leaders, considering mandates and the allocation of their time during the instructional day or after school hours. No matter the method, the overarching goal is to assemble people who have the will to mobilize others and lead sustainable change.

As a former school principal who implemented various recruitment methods without the support of a district DEI department, I highly recommend seeking initial interest through an opt-in method that requires you to fill in the gaps. If you have people who are willing to commit to complex work that requires creative and critical thinking, embrace it! If there are gaps in perspectives or low counts of participation, personally reach out to grade-level teams or departments to talk about the value a person can add to an equity team. For teachers pursuing administration, I would also highlight the vast leadership experiences that could be gained through one's participation in a team that analyzes educational systems. It makes a difference to have members who want to be present and engage in collective work through shared leadership.

Personal outreach to solicit team members does not mean coercing a member from a minoritized group to join an equity team. *Like seriously, please don't do it!* Although diverse representation is important and enhances decision-making processes with varied perspectives, people from minoritized groups should not feel pressured into joining an equity team solely because of how they identify. I have worked with schools where equity team members felt they were invited to participate because of their race or ethnicity. From a legal standpoint, you must also be cautious and conscious of any approach that can be discriminatory in nature. For instance, if a teacher of color was appointed against their will based on race and was subjected to mental health concerns as a result of topics discussed, that person could file a discrimination claim. Therefore, my outreach has involved personalized and humanizing conversations with grade-level teams, departments, or educators in pursuit of leadership roles.

As mentioned with caution, recruitment could also include the invitations of students and families connected to the school community. If a school lacks representation from different minoritized groups, extending an invitation to the community is also another option. Within an anti-DEI climate, you may have to strategically consider the language of the invitation to elicit different perspectives without directly saying: *Help! We are developing a team to promote inclusion and need people of color to join us!* Please consider the legalities and work with HR to understand ways to remain legally compliant in efforts to diversify teams. The community-based groups I devised as a principal, which specifically invited parents of color, did not pose liability to the district, considering the political climate nearly two decades ago and our board-approved partnership with Pacific Educational Groups, which guided that practice and model.

Legal compliance is important since the withholding of funding (as a result of anti-DEI policies) produces harmful consequences for students. As a result of executive orders or policies that call for the dissolvement of DEI language at federal or state levels, the names of equity teams may have to be considered as previously stated. Consult with your school district's attorney for current liability information. While making changes to abide by laws, we must remember that there is nothing wrong with DEI language. Equity work and practices that acknowledge the identities and histories of children are not inappropriate. The real problem is the dehumanizing beliefs of policymakers and their dismissal of efforts that support all children. If you choose to incorporate families and your equity team is not structured in a way to violate privacy rights, Figure 4.2 illustrates an example invitation to extend to families:

It is powerful to incorporate the voices of students and families in strategies to advance equity. School leaders must consider the roles of students and families who will serve on teams prior to recruitment methods. In other words, what do equity teams want families to do? What authority will families or students have on a school-based equity team? Is it possible for community members or students to implement all the measures that are outlined within a strategic plan? DEI practitioners can support school leaders to think about ways families and students can have meaningful engagement within equity teams. Figure 4.3 lists specific ways families and students can support school-based equity teams.

Example Recruitment Letter for School-Based Equity Teams
Dear Families, *Our school is developing a coalition that is designed to support the academic and social well-being of students. You may be familiar with our school's strategic plan for student achievement. You can find the strategic plan* ***linked here.*** *We have identified specific areas of focus to support positive student outcomes and would appreciate your voice to understand existing perceptions about our progress and strategies toward improvement. This coalition aims to build a bridge between our school and community. We hope participants will work in partnership with us to be a part of efforts that inspires a culture where all students thrive. The coalition will work to address the following:* • *Review and discuss progress as well as strategies toward student achievement.* ***(add content here that aligns with your school/district's mission)*** • *Promote a safe school climate.* ***(add content here that aligns with your school/district's mission)*** • *Foster a sense of belonging among members of our school community.* ***(add content here that aligns with your school/district's mission)*** *As a school that represents diverse cultural backgrounds, languages, and experiences, we welcome participants who can commit to the work of supporting all students. It is important for the coalition to have participants who can contribute perspectives that foster an inclusive environment and school community. If this collaborative effort interests you, please contact (****insert point of contact****) who will send you information about the upcoming meetings. Our first coalition meeting will be on (****insert date****) at (****insert location****). We look forward to your participation.* *Sincerely,* *Principal (add name of principal)*

Figure 4.2 Example recruitment letter for school-based equity teams.

Accountability

School-based equity teams operate more effectively in a culture of accountability. Every member of the team should feel empowered to contribute ideas, identify barriers, and make progress toward goals. Accountability requires systems to measure growth and the collective actions or behaviors of participants. If a school has established a strategic plan or initiatives to address disparities, accountability calls for a revisiting of goals and monitoring of progress. When needs assessments are conducted, and information is gathered, actions to improve services, organizational structures, and policies should follow. If 'standing on business' was a group, it *should* be an equity team. School-based equity teams should commit to action, own individual and collective responsibilities, and have systems to ensure desired outcomes.

<table>
<tr><th colspan="2">School-Based Equity Teams: Ideas for Meaningful Stakeholder Engagement</th></tr>
<tr><th>Students</th><th>Families</th></tr>
<tr><td>

- **Conditions for learning:** Students can identify the conditions they need for learning and engagement within classroom environments.
- **Culture and climate:** Students can discuss measures needed for an identity-affirming environment, including aspects that support emotional and physical safety.
- **Programming:** Students can discuss programming ideas to strengthen leadership, connections, and advocacy skills. They can also provide feedback regarding programs and initiatives.
- **Teacher feedback:** Equity teams can consider systems for teacher feedback that incorporate the voices of students.

</td><td>

- **Feedback:** Families can identify the strengths of a school community and areas of opportunity as related to a district or school's strategic plan.
- **Programming:** Families can also provide feedback regarding programs and initiatives.
- **Partnerships:** School leaders can identify areas of need and work with families to acquire partnerships with community organizations or businesses to advance goals. There are many untapped resources that exist in a community, and families may be affiliated with community-based groups that can help.

</td></tr>
<tr><th colspan="2">Students, Families, and Community Stakeholders
(e.g., businesses, organizations, etc.)</th></tr>
<tr><td colspan="2">

- **Policy work:** Stakeholders can review policies to determine how they may benefit or harm a community.
- **Inclusive community events:** Relationships are cultivated through community-building activities. Community members can work to plan events or festivities that promote a sense of belonging and inclusion.
- **Promotion of school-wide initiatives:** Stakeholders can be a part of the development of school-wide initiatives that help with accessibility, school funding, or components of a district's strategic plan (ex. math family game nights to support academic goals).
- **Professional development:** All stakeholders can contribute to professional learning experiences for school staff (ex. parent or student panels).
- **Physical environment:** Stakeholders can provide recommendations or resources to support or transform the layout, design, and space of school environments.

</td></tr>
</table>

Figure 4.3 School-based equity teams: ideas for meaningful stakeholder engagement.

Earlier in this chapter, I described an equity team's intent to assess the fidelity of schoolwide SEL initiatives. Through discussions with grade-level teams, it was apparent that SEL implementation was not consistent throughout classrooms. Some teachers shared that they lacked time to teach SEL curriculum as a result of instructional schedules. This claim launched the equity team into a discussion about time and how SEL could be integrated into other content areas. The equity team strived to eliminate barriers in efforts to hold everyone accountable for SEL instruction. To take it a step further, I also advised for the implementation of an accountability log or a tool where teachers could document completed lessons from the curriculum (e.g., many existing SEL curricula have tools for the documentation of lessons). If they wanted to thoroughly measure the correlation between discipline data and SEL curriculum, then a system of accountability was needed.

Protocols or community agreements can provide ground rules to ensure purposeful work, collegiality, and effective meetings. It is important to have expectations that guide a group's productivity and behaviors in a space conducive to critical conversations. Members of school-based equity teams can talk about their goals and set guidelines for how they will work together and communicate as a group. We know that labeling a space as 'safe' does not make it a 'safe space.' We must cultivate environments where people can be vulnerable and build trust. When I initially participated in equity teams as a teacher, I was accustomed to using *The Four Agreements* from the book, *Courageous Conversations About Race* (Singleton & Linton, 2006). Over time, I have shifted to use the following protocols listed in Figure 4.4 for my work within schools:

School-based teams can also develop systems of accountability to monitor their progress outside of the scope of school improvement goals.

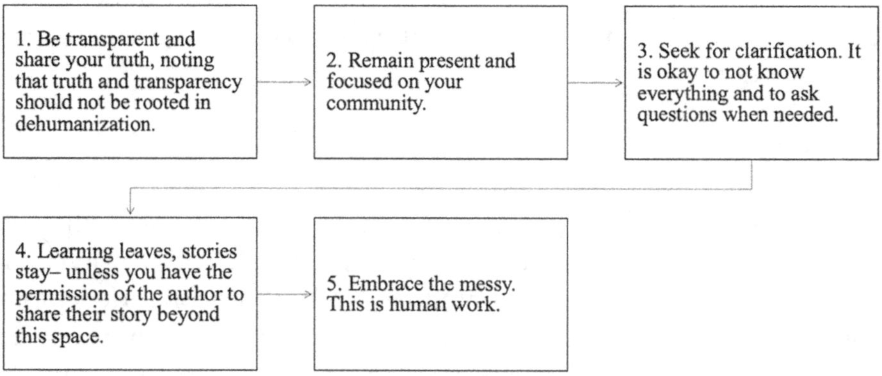

Figure 4.4 Protocols for shared learning and critical conversations.

Participants can revisit protocols or agreements to determine if their teams have a culture where people commit to actions and feel free to speak truth. I have worked with teams that perceived their work as unproductive due to fear of vulnerability. If teachers did not have a trusting relationship with their principal, they would not dare to assert the systems or practices that needed to change. An assessment of group dynamics is critical. If everyone is afraid to take risks and be honest, then the movement of an equity team will remain stagnant.

Self-assessments can also be helpful in guiding a team's effort. Teams can use a tool to assess their collective work at the beginning, middle, and end of the year. Appendix C is an evaluative tool that teams can use to assess their efforts. It provides criteria for measuring positive student relationships, leadership, pedagogical and data-driven practices, community engagement, and physical environments. The incorporation of evaluative tools can push teams to have deeper conversations about observable practices, evidence, and instructional needs.

Finally, the most important driver of accountability is the school principal. Accountability requires equity-focused leadership. Teams collapse when individuals are not mission-focused and leadership is lacking. For school-based teams, it is important for principals to demonstrate their commitment to educational equity. When leadership and clarity do not exist, school leaders invite frustrations and confusion into the group dynamic, losing champions over time.

Terri, a former Director of Equity and Inclusion from a suburban district in Indiana, met regularly with representatives of equity teams from each of the schools in her district. Oftentimes, teacher representatives would report that they were not granted the power or authority to implement the strategies outlined in their goals and shared how accountability systems did not exist. Per Terri, most teams were a check box for inclusion and did not lead to transformative work. Equity teams thrive with intentional leadership where principals make their commitment to equity visible through their presence, words, and actions.

Time and Compensation

Another consideration for school-based equity teams is the time and schedule of meetings. School leaders need to decide how often the team will convene and when participants will meet. There are school districts that have built-in time before or after school for committees and professional development. This means that learning opportunities or meetings occur within contractual hours, which may make planning easier for meetings. Some school districts may not have a structure where participants can work within contractual hours. Therefore, if teachers are required to work beyond contract hours (e.g., meetings whether in-person or virtual, school events, etc.), a school leader needs to consider how equity team members will be compensated for their time. This also underscores the importance of working in a school district or school that has a budget for DEI-related work.

School Improvement vs. Equity Teams

Most schools have more than one committee that focuses on student achievement. It is common to have school improvement teams that have goals tied to state or other accountability metrics. Oftentimes, I have been asked by principals to distinguish the difference between a school improvement committee and an equity team. Traditionally, school improvement teams (SITs) monitor strategies related to school improvement plans (SIPs). Although SIPs have goals related to school culture and climate (e.g., attendance, discipline, etc.), most plans heavily center academic achievement.

An equity team aligns its efforts with SIP goals but often delves deeper into the root causes of disparities and analyzes systems. Equity teams rigorously examine the impact of climate, organizational culture, and belonging on academic outcomes. For instance, a school improvement team may discuss strategies for reading comprehension, while the equity team may delve into the conditions students need to adhere to comprehension strategies (e.g., seating arrangements within the classroom, culturally responsive texts, etc.). In my experience in various contexts, school improvement teams have not been spaces where conversations about justice are normalized; and it's important to note that it does not have to be this way.

Any school-based team designed to support children should include teachers and staff who are committed to mirror work and advocacy for educational equity. SITs should emulate the practices of effective equity teams by explicitly addressing culturally responsive strategies, racial disparities, and underlying causes of inequities. It should be a team that leans into vulnerable conversations about educational justice, where members critically examine systems rather than brainstorming new programs or evaluating initiatives. If a school improvement team reflects or evolves into a group that carries a lens for equity in strategy development, both teams may not be needed.

Some school districts have distinct plans for the advancement of racial equity, perhaps in addition to SIPs. In those contexts, a separate team of equity-minded individuals may be beneficial to oversee specified goals. I have worked with principals who developed committees on top of committees (e.g., culturally responsive teaching committee, equity team, SIT, SEL committee, etc.) to address identical goals. To improve organizational efficiency, I advised leaders to merge multiple committees into one or two cohesive teams. Choose a route that leads to productivity and the reduction of burnout. DEI practitioners can also work with school leaders to determine a structure that meets their educational needs.

District Equity Leadership Teams

District equity leadership teams supervise the execution of strategies, programming, and progress toward goals throughout all divisions of a school district (Singleton, 2013). This team provides a vision and roadmap for equitable practices. District equity leadership teams require the visibility, leadership, and involvement of superintendents. When the highest position of power is intricately involved in the learning, discussions, and monitoring of equity work, it sends a strong message about prioritization of equitable practices. Here are key areas of focus for district equity teams:

- **Infrastructure for equity work:** Equity leadership teams set a vision for equity work and develop structures for learning, progress monitoring, self and systems assessments, staff and community engagement, and initiatives for school improvement.
- **Elimination of disparities across systems:** Equity leadership teams activate districtwide efforts to address disproportionality in data and identity threats in schools. Topics of discussion may include discipline referrals across divisions, disproportionality in enrollment in AP and honor courses, achievement disparities, community outreach, civil rights and anti-discriminatory practices, the implications of policies on equitable outcomes, and other relevant areas of need.
- **Ensuring students have access to high-quality instruction:** Equity leadership teams can analyze instructional systems, providing guidance to departments in their efforts to improve achievement outcomes for students.
- **Policy development:** Members of the district equity leadership team can determine a process to critically examine, revise, or develop district policies that impact schools.
- **Recruitment, retention, and wellness:** District equity leadership teams can consider strategies for the recruitment and retention of teachers as well as hiring or onboarding practices. Staff wellness can also be addressed in a systemic way to improve productivity.

Potential Participants District Leadership Team
1. Superintendent (Required) 2. Assistant Superintendent 3. Directors or officers (e.g., DEI, curriculum, special education, student services, multilingual learners, academic officer, etc.) 4. Principals 5. Specialists (e.g., instructional coaches, etc.) 6. Teacher or staff representatives (including association members) 7. School board member 8. Students 9. Parents or caregivers 10. Community-based educational experts (may not have a direct connection to a district, but can help through their expertise)

Figure 4.5 Potential participants for school-based equity teams.

Similar to school-based teams, it is impactful to have a diverse representation of leaders and staff on a district equity leadership team. DEI practitioners who serve as district administrators must ensure that people from different departments and school divisions are represented. Members will also need to determine norms and agreements for their work, as well as metrics to measure behaviors of the group dynamics and outcomes. Figure 4.5 lists potential participants for a district leadership team.

For some teams, it may be helpful to develop areas of focus where leaders are assigned to a priority goal that aligns with their strengths and interests. Focus areas can inspire intentional, small-group work to accomplish tasks and strengthen connections among leaders and staff across divisions or departments. The American Association of Colleges and Universities (AAC&U) promoted Inclusive Excellence (IE), a framework for integrating DEI work into an institution's core practices. After studying many Inclusive Excellence Plans from numerous universities, I developed a Systems Work framework with dimensions of liberatory work in schools and areas of focus. The dimensions of liberatory work in schools are the following:

1 **Individual:** the fostering of professional and personal growth within each working member of an institution
2 **Institutional:** systems work to improve practices, policies, and outcomes for students, faculty, and staff
3 **Instructional:** pedagogical approaches, curriculum, and instructional materials used to advance student achievement
4 **Intercultural engagement:** the work of building connections, a sense of community, and movements of empowerment

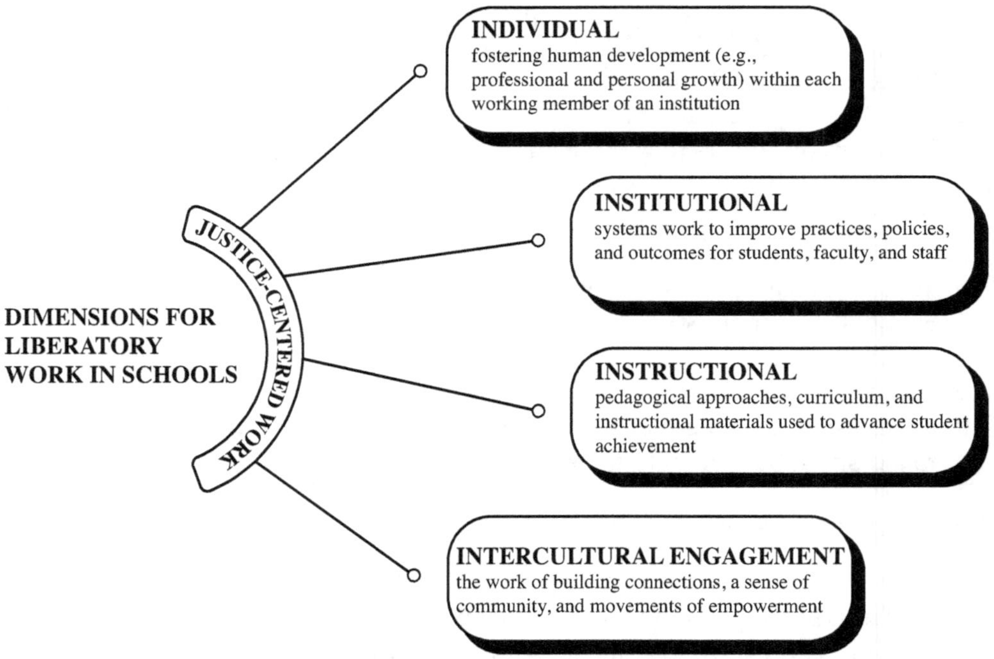

Figure 4.6 Dimensions for liberatory work in schools.

The identified areas of focus denote objectives that a district equity leadership team is expected to achieve or maintain. These areas of focus purposefully align with the dimensions of liberatory work in schools (Figure 4.6):

- **Community Partnerships and Engagement** (Intercultural Engagement)
- **Learning and Development** (Individual/Instructional)
- **Climate and Hiring** (Institutional)
- **Accessibility and Equitable Opportunities** (Institutional)
- **Diversity in the Curriculum/Co-Curriculum** (Instructional)

Appendix D has helped me to shape efforts, responsibilities, and the directionality of equity work in school districts. The dimensions cover both mirror and systems work, and the areas of focus emphasize actions that improve the climate and culture of school communities. I have been a part of district equity teams as a teacher and principal, where I felt inspired by conversations but did not necessarily do anything following the meeting. This framework was created to prioritize actions. No matter how you organize your meetings, ensure that everyone understands the objectives, commitments, and follow-up actions. Each person on the district equity leadership team can be influential in the work of building capacity for equitable practices in schools.

Equity Specialists

Building capacity may involve the expansion of DEI departments to include more staff with various areas of expertise. If you serve as a cabinet-level DEI practitioner within a large school district (serving 75,000 students or more), it may be helpful to review areas of growth and reimagine roles in education that can monitor and spearhead equity efforts across different divisions and schools. In larger school districts, it can be difficult for a DEI director to devote sufficient time to each school facility to effectively evaluate progress toward goals. Although district-level DEI practitioners may have access to a school's strategic plan, minutes of school-based equity teams, data, and progress monitoring tools, it does not compare to firsthand observations and consistent interactions with students as well as staff. Specialist roles under DEI departments can become another layer of supervision and support within schools. A person who specializes in a specific practice (e.g., Indigenous education, antiracism, community engagement, SEL, etc.) can help to optimize pedagogical approaches and conditions for learning. Specialists can partner with teachers, students, school administrators, community partners, and families to support strategies toward equity.

When I served as a Director of Equity and Inclusion in a metropolitan district with approximately 11,000 students, I had the following specialists in my department: *Coordinator of Community Partnerships and Student Programs (CCPSP), Social Emotional Learning (SEL) Coaches, and a High Ability Coordinator.* Each of those specialists reported to me and had the responsibility of working with either all schools or specific divisions. The CCPSP supervised all the school-based social workers and orchestrated resources for students as well as support for mental health. SEL coaches were assigned to a division (e.g., elementary, middle, and high school). They coached teachers, supported the delivery of SEL instruction, and fostered neuroscience education within schools. The high ability coordinator monitored disproportionality in enrollment and worked in partnership with me to develop inclusive programming models, such as clustering.

In Jefferson County Public Schools, a district that serves over 90,000 students, there are several specialist roles, such as the Generalist of Black Male Achievement, the Student Equity and Engagement Coordinator, and pedagogists. Each person plays a critical role in assisting and implementing strategies toward student achievement. All specialists work closely with the Chief

Equity Officer, a district executive leadership role. Specialists can use their gifts and expertise to advance collective efforts toward equitable practices.

When I started my first DEI role, I was a part of a small group of four people, known as the Student Success Team. However, I often felt isolated while working in a different department (HR) from teammates and having no thought-partners who could relate to my work. I felt compelled to create an infrastructure for equity work that would streamline communication and build capacity throughout the district. Once equity teams were established in each school, I asked principals to submit the names of participants who were strong facilitators, champions, and coordinators of DEI work. Those individuals, two from each school building, eventually became compensated as equity coaches through my advocacy.

The equity coaches kept me abreast of progress related to school-based strategic plans. They facilitated professional development experiences at the building and district level (see Professional Development in this chapter). Equity coaches were also transparent when leaders hindered efforts out of fear of community backlash. As mentioned, my first job was in a predominately white, conservative community that petitioned against DEI efforts long before federal and state-level policy changes. The equity coaches identified key areas for leadership development, which subsequently informed relevant learning opportunities.

Several equity coaches discussed how leaders and teachers were not equipped to have critical conversations. Therefore, I orchestrated a series of mandatory workshops via Teaching Tolerance (changed to Learning for Justice) where facilitators empowered educators to practice courageousness. School leaders and teachers participated in scenario-based learning exercises designed to encourage critical reflection on their approaches to managing conflict. Those opportunities were possible because of equity coaches' feedback and their assessment of needs. Appendix E is a mockup of the roles and responsibilities of equity coaches that could be altered for the development of any specialist position. Remember, new (potential) roles must be reviewed by district leadership, approved by the superintendent, and authorized by the school board.

There are districts that may not have a robust DEI-related department or cabinet-level positions to lead justice-centered work across schools and divisions. Therefore, many school districts may only have coordinators, coaches, or consultants to guide strategies toward achievement and identity-affirming environments. No matter the title or position, the role needs to be proximate to district leadership and in spaces where impactful decisions are made. As indicated in *Chapter 3*, it is a major red flag to be the only person in a department without power or a budget. Sometimes, we must advocate for additional staff or collaboration to avoid working in isolation. Specialist roles can be a part of collaborative work to address the dimensions for liberatory work in schools (Figure 4.6).

Building District-Level Community Coalitions

Although school-based equity teams may include families or community partners, it is critical for school district leaders to also build coalitions with external stakeholders to guide initiatives, practices, and policy work (Figure 4.7). Community coalitions invite families and local businesses or non-profit organizations to work in partnership with district administrators and school staff. These coalitions can also become an entity of advocacy that facilitates community-based education and rallies voices for institutional or structural changes. District-sponsored community coalitions require the participation and involvement of central office leadership, particularly superintendents. To build a community coalition, DEI practitioners should consider the following steps:

1 **Define the purpose of the coalition.** District leadership, including the superintendent, should define the components of a strong community-district partnership.

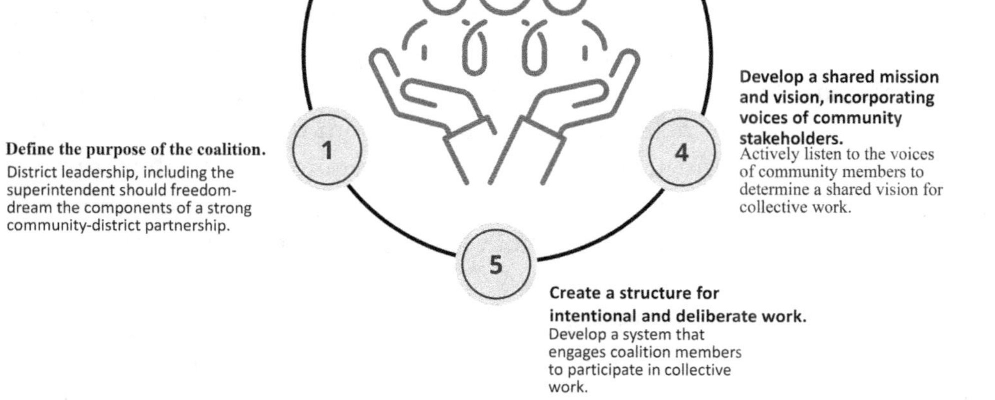

Figure 4.7 Building a community coalition.

2 **Define commitments.** Determine the expectations of district leaders and decide who will attend meetings or events related to the community coalition.
3 **Determine a structure for recruitment.** Consider a comprehensive approach for the recruitment of members that incorporates a diverse representation of community stakeholders. Similar to equity teams, there are different ways to recruit members of a community coalition. The purpose could be defined in a district publication (e.g., newsletter, flyer, virtual advertisement on social media, etc.), listing a point of contact for families who have an interest in joining. Another approach is through personal outreach. I have asked principals in both experiences as a DEI administrator to send me the names of parents or caregivers who would offer impactful feedback and perspectives on a community coalition. I personally reached out to those families. An 'invite-a-friend' method, encouraging participants to bring someone new to each session (perhaps with the incorporation of incentives) is also helpful once meetings have commenced.
4 **Develop a shared mission and vision, incorporating voices of the community.** Actively listen to the voices of community members to determine a shared vision for equity work. It is powerful when the community can come together to draft a mission and define how they will use their collective power to impact the lives of children.
5 **Create a structure for intentional and deliberate work.** Develop a system that engages coalition members to actually do work. No one wants to sit in a meeting and leave feeling unproductive. Provide members with an opportunity to get up and do something.

When I resigned from my first DEI role, I previously shared that I joined a metropolitan district as a DEI director. I started my role on the same day of the district's new community coalition meeting. The district worked with an educational consultant prior to my hiring who organized a diverse group of participants, which included representation from the local chapter of the NAACP, professors, directors of non-profit organizations, and other community partners. Many of these representatives were parents or caregivers of school children, while others were not connected to the district and wanted to support schools.

The first meeting included introductions and a conversation that prompted participants to reflect on strengths as well as opportunities for growth within the district. I documented the discussion about strengths and deepened the conversation about the opportunity gaps, encouraging members to explicitly name what needed to be improved. We shifted into a phase of productive struggle, identifying areas of focus for the coalition's work. After weeks of becoming more acclimated with the district, I learned that some of the opportunity gaps listed were things that leaders were actively doing. Discussions within coalition meetings demonstrated that our district needed to be more strategic in telling our story. We needed to help our community understand the strategies that were activated to address disparities.

To determine a mission and vision for the coalition, I encouraged community members to fill out a form where they submitted words, phrases, or statements to describe what our shared purpose could be as a collective. Through the language of the coalition and a thematic analysis, the Coordinator of Community Partnerships and Student Programs (CCPSP) and I developed a vision and mission statement that was edited and agreed upon by the group. The coalition determined that in partnership with schools and families, they would *aspire to be a force of advocacy in pursuit of a more equitable and inclusive community where educational outcomes are not predicted by socioeconomic status, race, gender, ability, or any other relevant social factor.* They wanted to build a bridge between families and schools in effort to provide an affirming educational experience for all children.

When involving families and community partners in collaborative work with school and district leaders, there must be an established structure that compels people to do something—*especially when you are inviting highly motivated people to co-construct solutions to inequities.* Community members identified many opportunity gaps based on data and their experiences within the school district. I organized the opportunity gaps into the following buckets to channel strategic planning and actions:

- **Connection and outreach:** This area of focus centered the work of building connections and helping families plug into DEI initiatives within the school district.
- **Equity and access:** This area of focus charged coalition members to examine the structural barriers that existed in communities that impacted access to resources, programs, or educational opportunities.
- **Civic action:** This area of focus inspired members to engage in policy work at a state or local level. It empowered coalition members to address a particular cause or need within the community.

Community coalition meetings often started with celebrations of student learning and updates from district administrators. Sometimes students would participate to present initiatives from advocacy clubs or to showcase their abilities. The areas of focus helped to narrow specific actions. For instance, many coalition members organized and attended the statehouse to denounce House Bill 1134 (Civic Action). Through the collective efforts and advocacy of several organizations, including the coalition, Indiana became the first red state to not pass anti-CRT legislation in 2022. The provision of focus areas is one way to shape collective work among community stakeholders. No matter the method of organizing a coalition, the approach and purpose should center the voices, humanity, and the empowerment of communities. Figure 4.8 takes a deeper look into the areas of focus developed for community coalitions. There are essential questions and potential actions that capture how community stakeholders can use their power. The mockup invitational letter (Figure 4.2), which describes the purpose school-based equity teams, could also be edited for the recruitment of coalition members.

Focus Areas for Community Coalitions		
Area of Focus	**Essential Question**	**Potential Actions**
Connection and Outreach	How can the school district improve connections and outreach to families within the school community?	• Development of community-based events or learning opportunities • Growing participation in parent-teacher organizations within schools
Equity and Access	How can the school district address access to resources and opportunities within schools and the community?	• Ensuring accessibility and accommodations at district-events (e.g., ASL, translators, etc.) • Fundraising efforts or school-drives for student resources
Civic Action	How can the coalition engage in civic action in ways that directly impact the school community?	• Organizing and advocating for just policies • Educating community members about the sociopolitical climate and educational legislation (ex. community members should know the connection between district budget cuts and state policies)

Figure 4.8 Focus areas for community coalitions.

Student Advocacy Groups

The development of student advocacy groups is another way to advance educational justice. In *Identity Affirming Classrooms: Spaces that Center Humanity,* I talk extensively about the purpose of student advocacy clubs with many narratives from youth. Students need outlets to build community and advocate for their needs. When students have spaces where solidarity exists, it can support identity development and generate a sense of belonging (Blomfield & Barber, 2009; Christison, 2013). DEI practitioners can encourage the creation of student advocacy groups (e.g., student council, student advisory boards, etc.) and work with students to gain qualitative data about their school experiences. I have facilitated sessions within student advocacy clubs to receive constructive feedback, explicitly asking students what lacks within schools and leadership. Additionally, I have supervised and worked with club sponsors (teachers and counselors) to offer learning opportunities and guidance for the growth of their organizations. If adults are striving to create a safe space for students, it is helpful to have a structure of collaboration where sponsors can connect, brainstorm ideas, and process scenarios that emerge from student discussions.

As a DEI Director, I also worked with club sponsors to develop a student leadership conference for all student participants within advocacy groups. The students were granted permission to go off-site during the instructional day to develop and enhance leadership skills. It was a full day of workshops facilitated by various community partners that were designed to focus on allyship, justice, and advocacy. Student advocacy groups can help to promote a climate where students take a stand against dehumanizing practices and walk in solidarity together.

Professional Development and Community-Based Education

The creation of purposeful learning opportunities can be a strategy for building capacity and knowledge among educators and community stakeholders. Professional learning experiences should not be seen as an event (Fisher et al., 2016), but rather an ongoing process that empowers a practitioner to be a better version of themself. It is important for staff to develop a critical consciousness (Freire, 2018)—*awareness of inequities and how power is used*—and a lens for justice that can be applied to their interactions and practices with colleagues, students, and families.

Throughout the years, I have developed and facilitated numerous professional learning experiences. To guide opportunities for learning and unlearning, I initially consider the beliefs or instructional gaps that are communicated through data. For instance, if students of color are omitted from high-ability programming, what lessons need to be learned about the ways we identify genius? What can we interrogate, research, and practice to become better educators for all children? The following questions help DEI practitioners to not only consider needs, but to think about the ways learning experiences and depth of knowledge can become the fabric of an institution. When professional learning is relevant, consistent, practiced, and tied to systems of accountability, it can significantly impact student outcomes.

Here are reflective questions for us to think deeply about professional learning experiences:

1 Which areas of focus need to be elevated in learning opportunities based on data or feedback from teachers or staff?
2 What learning experiences can be developed to match areas of focus or growth?
3 What lessons should people take away from the learning experience to inform and enhance their practices?
4 Who should people learn from? Do we incorporate multiple cultural perspectives in PD experiences?
5 How can learning experiences be embedded in the everyday lives of professionals?
6 How can learning experiences be integrated into accountability systems within a school or district?

Antiracist education has been a strong need in every institution where I have worked. Therefore, as a DEI practitioner, I intentionally developed partnerships with organizations that specialized in helping people understand structural and institutional forms of racism. In both districts of my employment, teachers were given many antiracist learning opportunities, including a powerful two-day intensive workshop called, Interrupting Racism. The organization known as Child Advocates walked participants through the shaping of racist ideologies that transcend into actions, systems, and policies. All administrators were required to attend these sessions.

Now, here's the difference between a district with equity-focused leadership and one that wants to check the inclusion box: *accountability for learned practices and outcomes*. When professional development is merely a check box, leaders will celebrate the staff completion rates of professional learning experiences over sustained learning and professional growth. Teachers can attend a workshop and leave with little to no takeaways. *This was a waste of my time.* Therefore, I am not impressed by completion rates, yet I am invested in coaching and systems for continued growth.

In my first DEI position, implementing systems of accountability proved challenging due to resistance from leadership. The absence of support made it difficult to ensure accountability. However, in my subsequent role, effective accountability systems were established through collective work. The knowledge from equity-focused professional learning experiences became an integral part of professional learning communities (PLCs). Educators were expected to name and discuss racial disparities as a part of norms for their collaborative work. District professional development days and teacher learning also centered the concept of building a critical consciousness (Freire, 2018). These professional learning experiences were co-planned by executive leaders who were a part of the Teaching and Learning division, including several directors and the assistant superintendent. Did everyone embrace antiracist pedagogy and implement it with fidelity? No. Were educational faculty and staff provided adequate coaching and held accountable? Yes. Instructional leaders (e.g., directors, coaches, assistant superintendents, etc.) worked together to conduct instructional walk-throughs and made their presence known within PLCs to ensure that professional learning lived within systems. This is an example of identifying a need, providing education, and embedding learned practices into systems of accountability.

Professional development can also be impactful when led by teachers, who have the ability to motivate peers more than any mandate could. In the article, *Planning Powerful Teacher-Led Professional Development* (2022), Jill Berg states that "teachers' rich knowledge of their school's students and families gives them an advantage when engaging colleagues in thoughtful action and reflection." In my first DEI role, equity coaches collaborated with me to develop a series called *Brave Conversations*. The equity coaches developed topics of interest and facilitated an afterschool series that was open to all employees within the district. Some of the sessions focused on immigration, multilingual learners, and supporting trans youth with the incorporation of student-parent panels. The messages of each session were clear, yet to the point of accountability, the learning experiences would have been more transformative with the support and presence of school and district leaders.

Community-based education is another way to foster growth and knowledge among stakeholders. We live in a society where many people advocate against DEI without being able to define it. Therefore, it is helpful for DEI practitioners to consider the education that community members need to understand a school district's commitment toward equitable practices. In my second DEI role, I conducted a webinar series during the height of COVID-19 called *Learning in Community*. The series hosted guest speakers who talked about social justice, gender diversity, high ability, and many other topics that were relevant within the school district. Parents from the community coalition facilitated one of the sessions and hosted Traci Baxley, who discussed principles from her book, *Social Justice Parenting* (2021). Parents and caregivers need opportunities to learn alongside others, ask questions, and clarify any misconceptions. Figure 4.9 lists some of my favorite professional

Books for Professional Growth and Human Development	
Books	**Author**
We Want to Do More Than Survive: Abolitionist Teaching and the Pursuit of Educational Freedom	Bettina L. Love
Equity Implementation: Case Studies and Practices for Educators and Leaders	Candice Dowd Maxwell and Andrea Brown-Thirston
Teaching to Transgress: Education as the Freedom Practice	bell hooks
Fix Injustice, Not Kids and Other Principles for Transformative Equity Leadership	Paul Gorski and Katy Swalwell
Leading Your School Toward Equity	Dwayne Chism
We Got This: Equity, Access, and the Quest to Be Who Our Students Need Us to Be	Cornelius Minor
The Racial Healing Handbook: Practical Activities to Help You Challenge Privilege, Confront Systemic Racism, and Engage in Collective Healing	Anneliese A. Singh
Recruiting and Retaining Culturally Different Students in Gifted Education	Donna Y. Ford
EmpowerED: A Roadmap for Navigating the Journey Towards Culturally Responsive Educational Practice	Renae Azziz
Teaching Fiercely: Spreading Joy and Justice in our Schools	Kass Minor
Cultivating Genius: An Equity Framework for Culturally and Historically Responsive Literacy	Gholdy Muhammad
The Little Book of Race and Restorative Justice: Black Lives, Healing, and US Social Transformation	Fania E. Davis
Antiracist Reading Revolution [Grades K-8]: A Framework for Teaching Beyond Representation Toward Liberation	Sonja Cherry-Paul
LGBTQ Youth and Education: Policies & Practices	Cris Mayo

Figure 4.9 Books for professional growth and human development.

development books that center racial justice, educational equity, and liberatory work in schools:

An Inside Look: How Do Other Schools Structure Their Equity Teams?

There are many ways equity-focused leaders can design and implement justice-centered work within schools. The structures I developed for equity work were based on my skills, the needs of the school communities, student populations, and the strengths of staff, many of whom were strong facilitators of learning and talented within their roles. Every work context is different, and the skill sets within teams may vary. Therefore, it is important to assess our environments and use our gifts in ways that make sense for our organizations. Here are other ways DEI practitioners have structured equity work within their school districts:

> *John Marshall, is the Chief Equity Officer of Jefferson County Public School district in Kentucky. He shared that the equity teams were mandated by the (previous) superintendent. The principal of each school could choose members of the team. An Equity Envoy, accompanied each equity team. The Envoy was a teacher who was paid extra to assist the school to make equity work fibrous. Equity Envoys were paid through the Diversity, Equity, and Poverty Department (DEP). It was their job to make sure equity work moved forward and to ensure that information, expectations, and needs were shared with each school through the DEP department.*
>
> *Penny Robbins is the Executive Director of Preschool of the Arts in Wisconsin. She does not separate DEI efforts into committee work. From her experience, a separate committee means that the work is being done by a few people and eventually becomes a separate entity from the work of the classrooms and administration. Therefore, she has been intentional to embed equity-centered practices in pedagogical work and administrative tasks to hold everyone on staff accountable for creating an inclusive, welcoming environment.*
>
> *Ayva Thomas leads inclusionary work in a district within the state of Washington. The leadership of equity teams are within individual schools. These teams were established as part of a broader effort to strengthen diversity, equity, and inclusion (DEI) at the school level. At the school level equity teams are primarily opt-in, with staff members and administrators, expressing interest based on their passion or experience with equity work. In some cases, team members were invited or recommended based on their leadership roles, lived experiences, or involvement in DEI initiatives. DEI practitioners aimed for diverse representation—across race, gender, roles in the school (teachers, counselors, classified staff, etc.), and perspectives. Most schools formed their*

teams more organically, through existing relationships and advocacy groups. There was a deliberate effort to ensure that the team did not consist solely of people already engaged in equity work but included skeptics or those newer to the conversation to broaden the impact. The equity team contacts generally meet four times a year. However, it differs from school to school and their core responsibilities vary.

Final Reflections Including Pitfalls to Avoid

Building capacity involves work that strengthens the abilities and leadership of people within an organization to achieve institutional goals. It requires a commitment from leaders to invest in the growth of members within an organization, fostering a culture of continuous learning. Every member of a school district should be knowledgeable of strategies, pedagogical approaches, and the dispositions needed to achieve equitable outcomes. Improving student achievement and belonging is a collective responsibility that must be integrated into accountability systems.

The various cadres or teams that were named in this chapter can be helpful but may not need to be a part of every school's story. Schools with a small quantity of staff members may not need an equity team—*in other words, their small, but mighty group is the team.* It may also be more feasible for district leaders to restructure the job descriptions of directors, rather than hiring new positions. If it is not possible to develop school-based equity teams, community coalitions, or specialist roles, continue to lean on thought partners and build coalitions with other schools or experts in the community for guidance. There are people within your reach who may be willing to support if you advocate for your needs.

Transparency and communication are key aspects of capacity-building approaches. When leaders are transparent about the goals and challenges of an institution, it inspires active participation and collective actions toward problem-solving. School communities, including teachers, staff, administrators, and stakeholders, must be aware of progress toward goals and have opportunities to engage in collective work in response to inequities. As stated by Penny Robbins, Director of Preschool of the Arts, teams or committees can become a hindrance if they become a separate entity that dissociates from a community. When teams or specialists become a secret society, the efforts—*no matter how hard people work*—do not yield to organizational change. No one wins if people are not working in community with each other. Educational staff can certainly serve as cheerleaders and motivators who spearhead DEI efforts, yet everyone must own the commitment to create environments that are conducive to learning and inclusion.

Chapter Highlights

1 It is important to build leadership capacity, ensuring that there is a shared responsibility for equity work.
2 The development of equity teams (school-based or district-level) or community coalitions requires an intentional approach for recruitment and collective work. A diverse representation of members across school divisions and communities will yield to the creativity and collaboration that is needed to build a pathway toward equitable outcomes.
3 Students have a comprehensive view of educational systems based on their lived experiences in schools. Through student advocacy clubs, educational leaders can learn about inequities through the lens of youth and co-construct action steps. Building capacity also means cultivating leaders for the next generation.
4 Professional development should be constructed based on the needs identified by staff, data, and the school community. Learning is not a one-and-done workshop but is rather an ongoing endeavor to strengthen the culture and practices within an organization. Accountability systems ensure that learning lives beyond a book club or an event and becomes a normalized practice.
5 Everyone is responsible for justice-centered work. No matter the infrastructure that is created to advance equity, each member of a school district should know their role in dismantling disparities.

Mirror Work

1 How do I define 'capacity building' in efforts to lead schools toward equity?
2 What support do I need to strengthen capacity-building approaches toward equity in schools?

Systems Work

1 What infrastructure is needed in my school district or school to advance equity work?

References

Azziz, R. (2024). *EmpowerED: A roadmap for navigating the journey towards culturally responsive educational practice*. Virtuoso Education Consulting.

Baxley, T. (2021). *Social justice parenting: How to raise compassionate antiracist, justice-minded kids in an unjust world*. Harpers College Publishing.

Berg, J. H. (2022). *Planning powerful teacher-lead professional learning*. ASCD. https://ascd.org/blogs/planning-powerful-teacher-led-professional-learning

Blomfield, C. J., & Barber, B. L. (2009). Brief report: Performing on the stage, the field or both? Australian adolescent extracurricular activity participation and self-concept. *Journal of Adolescents, 32*(3), 733–739.

Cherry-Paul, S. (2024). *Antiracist reading revolution [Grades K-8]: A framework for teaching beyond representation toward liberation*. Corwin.

Chism, D. (2022). *Leading your school toward equity*. ASCD.

Christison, C. (2013). The benefits of participating in extracurricular activities. *BU Journal of Graduate Students in Education, 5*(2), 17–20. https://files.eric.ed.gov/fulltext/EJ1230758.pdf

Davis, F. (2019). *The little book of race and restorative justice: Black lives, healing, and US Social transformation*. Good Books.

Fisher, D., Frey, N., & Hite, S. A. (2016). *Intentional and targeted teaching: A framework for teacher growth and leadership*. ASCD.

Ford, D. (2013). *Recruiting and retaining culturally different students in gifted education*. Routledge Publishing.

Friere, P. (2018). *Pedagogy of the oppressed*. 50th Anniversary Edition. Bloomsbury Academic.

Gorski, P. & Swalwell, K. (2023). *Fix injustice, not kids and other principles for transformative equity leadership*. ASCD.

hooks, b. (1994). *Teaching to transgress: Teaching as the freedom practice*. Routledge Publishing.

Love, B. (2019). *We want to do more than survive: Abolitionist teaching and the pursuit of educational freedom (2019)*. Beacon Press.

Maxwell, C. & Brown-Thirston, A. (2023). *Equity implementation: Case studies and practices for educators and leaders*. Rowman & Littlefield.

Mayo, C. (2014). *LGBTQ youth and education: Policies & practices*. Teachers College Press.

Minor, C. (2019). *We got this: Equity, access, and the quest to be who our students need us to be*. Heinemann Publishing.

Minor, K. (2023). *Teaching fiercely: Spreading joy and justice in our schools*. Jossey-Bass.

Muhammad, G. (2020). *Cultivating genius: An equity framework for culturally and historically responsive literacy*. Scholastic.
Singh, A. (2019). *The racial healing handbook: Practical activities to help you challenge privilege, confront systemic racism, and engage in collective healing*. New Harbinger Publications.
Singleton, G. (2013). *More courageous conversations about race*. Corwin Press.
Singleton, G. & Linton, C. (2006). *Courageous courageous conversations about race*. Corwin Press.

5

Cultivating a Responsive and Inclusive Work Culture

The identity of a school district or school is shaped by its culture (Gruenert & Whitaker, 2015). A work culture reflects the beliefs, values, and behaviors within an environment. Culture influences what we do and how we respond in school spaces. Within educational contexts, culture guides the language we use and forms norms that are socially acceptable. Many of us are familiar with terms such as *best practice* and *professional learning communities* because of the culture of educational contexts. The culture of a school conveys an "unwritten mission" (Gruenert & Whitaker, 2015, p. 30). Although mission statements and strategic plans communicate the purpose of our work, culture reveals how we show up and whether we are aligned to the guiding principles of an organization.

Many school districts develop vision and mission statements that emphasize appreciation for diversity, belonging, inclusion, and equity, yet the culture within the institution may convey a different reality. Although school and district statements indicate a commitment to inclusionary work, human interactions, professional practices, and leadership decisions may make a vision feel more rhetorical than foundational. Culture often reveals a disconnect between what is promoted and what is practiced. Teachers may experience exclusion in districts that promote inclusion, and students may be denied opportunities from schools that emphasize the importance of equal access. The gaps between vision, core values, and culture can produce tension, damage trust, and undermine a school's credibility.

An inclusive school culture does not automatically generate from an organization's statement of core values or vision and mission statements. It takes

DOI: 10.4324/9781032623542-5

intentional leadership to shape school cultures with the premise that all students, staff, and families hold value. Although inclusion is a desirable outcome within an organization, it is also the bare minimum to generate a space of belonging. Educational leaders must build capacity for introspective work, anti-bias and anti-racist education, humanizing practices, civic discourse, and just systems.

As DEI practitioners, we have the unique responsibility of cultivating equity-focused leadership. This involves collaboration with school and district leaders to develop shared commitments and knowledge pertaining to justice-centered work. One of the most critical partnerships DEI practitioners can establish is with school principals. School leaders are vital and influential in the work of fostering cultural shifts for positive student outcomes. Changing a culture "requires knowledge of where a school has been, and agreement about where the school should go" (Muhammad, 2018, p. 25). Principals [should] have a strong pulse of their schools, including the policies, pedagogical approaches, and interactions that shape a school's culture and the experiences of students. Their understanding of a school's needs and challenges is valuable and can guide the work of DEI practitioners.

Leading cultural shifts within an organization or school is not an easy feat. It is difficult to move people in the same direction who uphold different belief systems. Anthony Muhammad (2018) reminds us in his book *Transforming School Culture: How to Overcome Staff Division* that we are not in the business of mind control and cannot coerce people into an improved school culture where everyone holds shared values. A tyrannical approach to leadership does not benefit the growth of teachers, educational leaders, or staff, but rather degrades them and the profession more. Paulo Freire (2022) also conveyed in *Pedagogy of the Oppressed* that "when people are already dehumanized, due to the oppression they suffer, the process of their liberation must not employ methods of dehumanization (p. 67)." It is no secret that many educators struggle with their worth and value while existing in a society that constantly devalues and criticizes our work. Therefore, we cannot bulldoze and insensitively push people into the work of cultivating an inclusive and responsive culture. A profound approach is needed to achieve cultural change, and it starts at the individual level with each of us holding a mirror.

Doing 'All the Things' with Little Results: What Is Missing?

When data indicates a need for improvement, educational leaders are compelled to develop technical solutions. For instance, let's examine and make a mental checklist of methods to improve reading outcomes at an elementary school. If reading instruction is an area of growth across grade levels, there may be measures put in place ranging from professional development to adjustments with instructional practices. Administrators may conduct instructional rounds during reading blocks and provide real-time feedback. *Check.* Teachers may participate in professional learning communities and talk about strategies to improve decoding and comprehension skills. *Check.* Parents and caregivers may be invited to events that allow them to participate in literacy experiences. *Check.* School leaders may host nights where families learn about reading data and strategic plans. *Check.*

There are several technical solutions we can implement to address one specific problem. The problem-solving process can often feel like a game of darts. There are targets we must meet to achieve goals, and it often feels like we are throwing a ton of strategies on a board that constantly miss the mark. Technical solutions, such as changing schedules, grading practices, and community events, are helpful and can produce incremental gains. However, there are many initiatives that are not sustainable and fail to address the root of the problem.

In my consulting and professional work experiences, I have often heard people refer to their districts as a *jack of all trades and master of none.* By the time teachers get acclimated with a particular program or curriculum, it is in the process of being phased out. People are experiencing burnout while striving to prioritize student learning and balancing multiple initiatives. Meanwhile, the new educational trends, ongoing training, and pressures to improve data can still potentially yield to disadvantageous outcomes. When educators are working relentlessly to implement multiple strategies and progress toward student achievement remains stagnant, we are left with one question: What is missing?

I worked with a teacher who was responsible for a course that focused on culture and social justice. This course was designed to teach students about the parallels between historical movements of the past and present. Therefore, themes of race, identity, and power were threads throughout each unit. After receiving course-related concerns from a parent and principal, I made it a practice to observe the classroom and partner with the teacher. Considering the political waves of anti-DEI rhetoric, my initial suspicion was that the complaints were a part of a larger agenda. The teacher was captivating, and it was obvious that the students appreciated his energy. However, I noted that an opportunity for critical dialogue among students was missing. Additionally, if students were asked to provide opinions about historical events, they often lacked key background knowledge that was not taught. The teacher's delivery of historical information also had gaps that led to confusion. It was a session where the teacher shared his thoughts and beliefs as truth, rather than presenting factual information and allowing students to draw their own conclusions.

The teacher and I met to debrief the instructional lesson. It was evident that he needed to spend more time unpacking the content, pedagogical approaches, and his beliefs to make the learning less biased and clear for students. Although the lesson plans could have been more defined, I was more concerned about the approach and delivery of instruction that was solely driven by beliefs. Instead of focusing on self-reflections during our debriefing session, he was more invested in discussion points about the tools he needed for the course. *What homework can I create? Which videos should I incorporate in class? Who should I tap into for guest speakers?* All of the questions were valid and necessary for curriculum development, and none of those resources addressed his beliefs that harmed the well-being of students and overshadowed learning experiences.

When thinking about this coaching opportunity and school improvement efforts that solely focus on technical solutions, the following thoughts come to mind:

- If we lead without self-awareness, then parts of our unconscious being can sabotage our efforts toward liberation.
- If we lead with ignorance, the strategies we embrace may not be productive or live up to our intentions.
- If we lead and lack a clear vision, we may commit to areas of focus that never address the real problem.

Belief systems are powerful. They influence our actions and how we approach situations in our everyday lives. Beliefs guide how we use tools and implement strategies. Our beliefs empower us to focus, commit, or withdraw from commissions. The visions that exist in school corporations are shaped by beliefs. We have a clarity of purpose from shared beliefs within educational systems. Beliefs inform us how to deal with obstacles and setbacks when challenges bring us back to the drawing board.

The promotion of educational equity is often impacted by belief systems. Our beliefs can either propel us forward, guiding us to take actions toward justice, or serve as a barrier, perpetuating inequities and hindering progress. The underlying beliefs we carry influence our leadership approaches, decision-making, and interactions. In the field of education, there is much time spent on the construction of solutions within schools and little time devoted to the deconstruction of our beliefs. If tools, resources, and strategies are not fostering inclusive school cultures or generating positive outcomes for students, perhaps we should restart the problem-solving process with a critical examination of our beliefs.

Mirror Work for Educational Leaders

As educational leaders, it is important for us to be reflective practitioners and to consider the shaping of our leadership. This calls for us to look in a mirror and speak truths about our own humanity and interactions with others. Mirror work is a powerful tool that helps us to learn more about our identity as humans and the experiences that guide how we lead. It encourages us to be self-aware as we explore our own beliefs, strengths, and interactions within the world. Mirror work also helps us to examine our emotional responses to happenings within society and educational systems. We can explore why we lean toward a particular side of an issue, and study what or who we acknowledge in the world.

Like many educators, I work hard to show up for my students yet struggle at times to pour into myself and my own human development. During busy weeks of wearing multiple hats, I may forget to slow down and ask myself, *Have I been a good human today?* As educational leaders, it is imperative to consider how we lead and how our leadership is perceived by others. Mirror work is a personal and ongoing introspective process. It is an intentional practice that I implement in my leadership and teach in my professorship. There are times when *life is lifing,* and I am not consistent with my mirror work, but I am generally committed to self-awareness and practices that push me to reflect on my leadership. When we identify things about ourselves that need growth and commit to change, we align closer to our values. Mindfulness of our being, communication, emotions, and approaches can support the development of conscious leaders.

Accountability is an act of care for ourselves and others. We should want to become better versions of ourselves and empower others to grow in their personhood and leadership. Mirror work is an accountability system that functions as an ethic of love. To love ourselves means that we must hold ourselves accountable. We must be willing to critique ourselves to foster personal growth and improvement. In bell hooks' book, *All About Love,* she discusses how awareness helps us to develop an ethic of love. When our leadership is not aligned with an ethic of love, we are not only harming the individuals we serve but are also robbing ourselves from our full humanity:

> *Embracing a love ethic means that we utilize all the dimensions of love-care, commitment, trust, responsibility, respect, and knowledge- in our everyday lives. We can successfully do this only by cultivating awareness. Being aware enables us to critically examine our actions to see what is needed so that we can give care, be responsible, show respect, and indicate a willingness to learn*
>
> (2001, p. 94).

Mirror work helps us to remain connected to our humanity. When we lack the will and ability to self-examine our personal thoughts and actions, we navigate and lead environments while being disconnected from truths that shape our identities (e.g., as teachers, principals, counselors, parents, etc.). We may work in schools with the belief that our leadership is making a positive impact and not realize that our view is limited or different from the thought bubbles of others. I have worked with educational leaders who claimed to have a good rapport with staff, and meanwhile, staff were counting down the days to their retirement and ready to cue up the song *No One Mourns the Wicked* as a part of their departure. This lack of self-awareness limits our ability to connect, grow, and hold others accountable. Mirror work is foundational to our leadership identity. We detach ourselves from our values and our humanity when we remove self-awareness from our practices.

During times when educational leaders congregate (e.g., leadership meetings, retreats, data reviews, etc.), it is impactful for DEI practitioners to create time and space for introspective work. The decisions we make as leaders are often driven by belief systems that need to be assessed. For example, dress code policies reflect the ways leaders have been socially constructed to believe what attire is acceptable. Disciplinary procedures provide insights of belief systems related to human behaviors (e.g., the ways we define disruption, disrespect, engagement, etc.). Educational leaders need more time for mirror work to understand their decision-making patterns, biases, and communication practices. When we pause to reflect on our impact and interrogate areas of growth, we not only strengthen our emotional intelligence but also model dispositions that motivate others to improve and respond to challenges productively.

In my leadership experiences as a DEI practitioner and an assistant professor, I intentionally promote mirror work among principals and aspiring educational leaders. As humans, we tell ourselves what is normal, socially accepted, or right as we operate in different spaces. We also create dominant narratives of what we consider as truth and carry it with us into workspaces. Mirror work invites us to deconstruct dominant narratives, deficit thinking, and beliefs that may contribute to educational conditions that elevate some children and confine others from reaching their full potential. Educational leaders (e.g., superintendents, directors, principals, instructional coaches, specialists, etc.) need built-in opportunities to wrestle with the beliefs that have influenced their approach to liberatory work. The following questions jumpstart mirror work for educational leaders. DEI practitioners are advised to examine the questions beforehand to reflect on their own leadership practices. For district-level DEI practitioners, whether participating in cabinet meetings or a designated session for administrators, I recommend selecting several targeted questions for educational leaders to collaboratively address

Mirror Work for School Leaders
Prior to the start of any meeting that involves mirror work, it is important to consider the protocols that are needed for vulnerable conversations. Identify what people need within an environment to fully participate and contribute to learning experiences. Provide each educational leader a notebook that is purposed as a leadership journal. Prior to the start of each meeting, select a question or two from the list provided or see Figure 5.2. Give 3–5 minutes of writing time where leaders can process their personal thoughts. Provide a brief time for collective sharing following the writing activity. Start with pairings, where leaders are partnered with another person to share their reflections. Then, open the dialogue to the whole group, asking pairs to share what may have been learned. Emphasize that leaders do not have to share personal or intimate details of self but encourage them to talk about their thought process. For instance, did the questions spark immediate thoughts, or was it challenging to generate responses? If it was challenging, could educational leaders talk about the reasons that made the question(s) difficult to answer? What are the leadership implications of the questions? Encourage leaders to reflect on the assigned question(s) following leadership meetings, asking them to write thoughts in their leadership journals. Encourage leaders to reflect on how their experiences are shaping their leadership and sense of self.

Figure 5.1 Mirror work for school leaders.

under your facilitation. Also, consider Figure 5.1, which shares a structured activity for introspective work and leadership development:

1. What is my identity as a leader?
2. What experiences have shaped my leadership identity?
3. Who has helped to shape my identity as a leader?
4. What are my values as a leader?
5. How do I walk in those values at work and within my everyday life?
6. What does it mean to be human?
7. How do I center the humanity of others in my leadership?
8. How do my leadership values align with my humanity?
9. How does racism operate within the district or school building?
10. What identity threats can I identify from school or district-based policies?

Mirror Work for School Leaders

Figure 5.2 helps us to become conscious, responsive leaders. We cannot be in a mode of doing and lack awareness of our actions, language, and the impact

Mirror Work Starter Kit Questions

Equity lens questions:

- How do I assess situations? (e.g., via bias, emotions, factual information, narratives, etc.)
- Whose voices am I centering as I work to resolve a problem?
- Do I examine and evaluate my beliefs, ideologies, and interactions with others after each workday or week?
- Can I identify educational inequities in my own building or department?
- Who benefits from the decisions I make in our school community?
- Who is harmed from the decisions I make in our school community?

Educational experience:

- What does it mean to be human?
- Who saw my full humanity in my Pre-K-12 experiences?
- Who cared for me authentically in Pre-K-12 environments?

Showing up for justice:

- What does racial equity, justice, and inclusion mean to me?
- How does the work of advancing equity show up in my practices?
- How does the work of advancing equity, dismantling racism, and creating inclusive, affirming environments show up in my everyday life?

Unpacking our power:

- How am I using my power to ensure that each student, family, and colleague feels a sense of belonging?
- How am I contributing to conditions where students feel safe and valued?
- How am I using my power to create systems and educational spaces where all students can thrive?
- How do I use my power to help parents/caregivers access the benefits my district or school offers?

Power of language:

- How do I empower students, families, or colleagues through the language I use in the workplace, classrooms, or other educational settings?
- How do I use my voice to name what harms educational institutions, children, or communities?
- How do I use my voice to say what needs to be said in the moment?

Marching forward:

- Do I have the will to engage in the deep work of dismantling oppressive structures in educational systems?
- How do I demonstrate courageousness?
- What excites me about the advancement of equity work in my organization?
- What personally holds me back from progressing educational justice?
- What do I need to become an equity-focused leader?

Figure 5.2 Mirror work starter kit questions.

of our decisions. We cannot be serious about the elimination of racial disparities and lack knowledge about the ways racism operates in systems or our own ideologies. Educational justice requires an analysis of power, beliefs, and leadership behaviors. As DEI practitioners, it is important to know where we and others stand on issues related to educational equity. We need opportunities to interrogate our practices and beliefs. We should be aware of the ways we show up to others, knowing what may be shared in a room when our presence is absent. If we lead with a pro-human approach, then we should care about the impact our leadership has on others. As educational leaders who are DEI practitioners, we need to know if we are contributing to the inequities we desire to dismantle.

We know that well-intentioned people can still cause harm. I have counseled numerous equity-minded teachers, including graduate students who have felt disheartened by the roadblock known as their school principal. When school leaders insist on the importance of supporting all students but contradict that messaging through their behaviors, it shapes the culture and reveals the emptiness of DEI initiatives that lack clear vision and purpose. For example, I was summoned to support a high school as a result of a tragic incident that involved a student stabbing another peer. I oversaw districtwide systems that promoted social-emotional learning (SEL), and supervised SEL coaches and a specialist who managed the systems of school-based social workers. The practices and concepts of SEL were not widely embraced in this high school based on ongoing feedback from coaches. While orchestrating systems of support, navigating trauma, and working with law enforcement on the day of the tragic incident, the principal approached me in front of a group of teachers and asked sarcastically, "You really think SEL will fix this?" My immediate response was, "Yes, among many other proactive measures, strategies, and structures that need to be in place." However, in the back of my mind, I knew that any strategy from my department would be doomed from the start, as a result of the principal's publicized deficit views about SEL and the scope of my work.

Mirror work helps us to shine a light on ourselves. Through the interrogation of practices and beliefs, we can begin to understand that some technical changes to systems may not be the answer. Sometimes the answer lies in the beliefs that fuel the strategies we use. Leading with integrity and modeling the cultural norms we aspire to achieve is contingent upon the beliefs we carry. Although it is difficult to look in the mirror and review aspects of ourselves, we need to understand our personal role in the movement of goals. Through ongoing mirror work, we gain clarity, thoughtful approaches to decision-making, and an understanding of how we show up into DEI work.

Exploring Shadow Work

When I think of my own leadership identity in DEI work, there are many people who come to mind who have empowered me to lead changes in systems. In my first book, I talked about a scholar and educator of over 60 years named Patricia Payne who inspired my passion for anti-racist pedagogy. She taught me the importance of owning my own story, using my voice, and walking in my truth. My entry point into the facilitation of DEI work resulted from her invitation to lead a workshop for a conference within Indianapolis Public Schools. Her faith in my knowledge, abilities, and will, deeply influenced my career path. I spoke with truth and conviction during the initial conference as an intern and undergraduate student, and I have not stopped talking since that opportunity. There will never be a time when I do not give Payne the flowers she deserves, yet I want to take an intentional pause to uplift another mentor named Courtlandt Butts.

I met Courtlandt Butts, a former educational consultant through Pacific Educational Group (PEG) in 2009. He conducted a Beyond Diversity training in the school district where I served as a kindergarten teacher. The district had a multiyear partnership, and I continued to learn from him as I matriculated into an assistant principal position and eventually became an elementary principal. Courtlandt was knowledgeable, approachable, and packaged hard truths in ways that were receptive to an audience. However, the most admirable quality about his facilitation was his humanizing approach. You were seen and connected through his words, and it felt like a gift to be in his presence. After the partnership dissolved, I did not see him again until ten years later as a DEI director in my second role. He was an independent consultant who was hired to provide an equity audit and executive coaching to support leaders within central office; and eventually extended services to building principals.

Given my past experiences with Courtlandt, I anticipated that he would provide administrators with resources to address racism and challenge whiteness in schools. I braced myself for the reactions within the room, anticipating body language that expressed discomfort. However, this time he focused on our common humanity. He asked administrators to introduce themselves by who they were as human beings, not job titles. Then, he encouraged the group to embrace a different component of self-introspection, known as shadow work.

Psychologist Carl Jung introduced the concept of shadow work in his book, *Anion* (1979). The shadow represents parts of our unconscious being (e.g., emotions, impulses, etc.) that require exploration to fully understand ourselves and our interactions in the world. We confront aspects of ourselves that may not be visible to our human psyche. Shadow work allows us to embrace parts of ourselves, including strengths and areas of growth, that we neglect to process or develop while navigating the moving parts (e.g., relationships, health, jobs, family, etc.) of life. For people who are navigating trauma or trying to heal emotional wounds, shadow work could be designed as an intensive strategy that is led by a licensed therapist. Yet, for leadership growth and development, using gentle techniques of shadow work to promote awareness is helpful.

Courtlandt asked administrators to consider their humanity and the beings they bring into workspaces. He asked us to think about our strengths, challenges, and what people would say if we were absent from a room. We were also encouraged to think about the things we needed to admit to ourselves and have avoided. Many of us expected to be a part of a training that focused on strategies and school-based solutions, yet we were left with more questions about our leadership and its relation to existing inequities. The most powerful aspect of this exercise was not what happened within the room, but the assigned tasks beyond the workspace.

Shadow work brings to light the hidden parts of ourselves. One of the most productive ways to make those hidden parts transparent is through critical conversations with people who interact with our everyday lives. We were asked to find individuals we knew well, who could have a courageous conversation with us about our strengths, areas of growth, and what people discuss about our leadership identity when our presence is absent. The criteria for the individuals included finding someone who generally aligned with our beliefs, and recruiting someone who was not afraid to challenge us and provide unfiltered truths—*two different types of people to assess our leadership.* This dynamic would allow for a wide range of perspectives to guide personal reflections.

Protocols for the discussion were also required and can be found in Figure 5.3. The individuals selected to answer questions about our strengths and areas of growth had to respond without any interruptions from us, the interviewers. We could not interject, state commentary in self-defense, or derail the conversation with new thoughts. Rather, we had to actively listen and hold space for the truths of others to promote our human development. The observations and feedback from peers did not define our humanity, but provided insights into the way we project our being or leadership to others.

In the book *Change Your Questions Change Your Life* (2015), author Marillee Adams asks, *How can you get the best answers without asking the best questions first* (2022, p. 23)? As educational leaders, the best questions are ones that force us to look at the shaping of our leadership and the systems we lead. They are questions that help us to understand how we use our power. Baruti Kafele (2018), educator and national speaker, often calls for educational leaders to ask themselves, "Is my school a better school because I lead it?" To answer

Shadow Work Practice for Leaders

During a moment of solitude, take the time to answer the following questions for yourself:

- What are my strengths as a leader? What are my challenges as a leader?
- What can people count on me for? What can people not count on me for?
- When have I demonstrated courageous leadership?
- What do I think people say about my character when I am not in the room?

After responding to the questions, find at least two individuals to interview. Each selected person will answer the same questions and describe their perceptions of you. This may take time to schedule.

Intentionally choose individuals who care for your being and know you well enough to add substance in their contributions. Also, consider selecting people who align with your beliefs or dispositions and individuals who may offer differing views or unfiltered truths. When I completed the exercise with Courtlandt, I chose an individual who would likely offer affirmations and a person who would feel unbothered critiquing me. You want well-rounded perspectives to understand the hidden aspects of yourself and should not select anyone who would put you in a volatile situation—*I stress that point heavily in my facilitation.*

At the scheduled time of the interview, explain to the person that you will ask them questions. Inform the interviewer that you want their unfiltered truth for your human and leadership development. Explain that you will ask a question and allow them to speak without any interruptions until their response is complete. After the completion of the response, you will be allowed to ask at least two clarifying questions to understand what was shared.

Continue these protocols until all questions have been asked. Make sure to show gratitude for the bravery and thoughtfulness of participants. Although it may not be easy to hear the truth, it is not easy for people to share criticisms either. This exercise also strengthens skills needed for critical conversations.

After the experiences, ask yourself the following questions:

- What did I learn about myself through this experience?
- What did I learn about my leadership?
- How did my personal beliefs of align with the views that were shared?
- What areas do I want to focus on for professional or human growth?

Make a personal plan for yourself to address areas of growth. You may want to revisit the participants from the dialogue and ask if they have suggestions for your path toward self-improvements. Remember to be kind to yourself as you process leadership areas you want to nurture.

Figure 5.3 Shadow work practice for school leaders.

this question, we must understand our leadership behaviors and how our actions yield to impact. When we identify areas of growth and intentionally change leadership behaviors, we change outcomes within schools.

Systems Work

Systems are made of interconnected parts that work together to produce outcomes. In educational settings, those parts include the policies, pedagogical practices, structures (e.g., schedules, funding, curriculum, assessments, etc.), programs, and relationship dynamics that yield to achievement and inclusive environments. While mirror work encourages us to reflect on our leadership identity, systems work calls for us to study the function, connections, and underlying issues of the educational parts that shape an institution. When we identify inequities, problems, or opportunity gaps, systems work invites us to examine the conditions or parts of an educational setting that create disparities. Through systems work, we address the root causes of problems, and work to dismantle and rebuild structures to promote values of justice—*fairness, human dignity, equal opportunities and protection of rights.* In DEI work, a just system reflects a common language for equity, structures for accountability, and the adoption of humanizing approaches.

Building a Common Language

In my first DEI position, I made the assumption that most people understood the purpose of my role. After listening tours and conversations with school leaders, I learned that many people did not understand the scope of my work nor the language I used to describe the cultural shifts that were needed in systems. Many people had different views on the definition of educational equity and the best ways to put it into practice. Some of the definitions solely focused on race, while other meanings emphasized the concept of equality. If leaders, particularly principals, struggled to articulate a clear definition, it would have been unrealistic to expect teachers and staff to understand the purpose as well as actions needed for the advancement of equity. When purpose, clarity, and direction lacks, accountability (an ethic of love to improve yourself and others) cannot live within systems.

As DEI practitioners, it is necessary to ensure that every member within an organization has an understanding of what equity means, including knowledge of institutional commitments and strategic plans to eliminate unjust practices. The language used in work environments influences and signals our behavioral responses (Gruenert & Whitaker, 2015). Furthermore, the words we use to describe our work and its purpose shape the culture of an organization. Words hold power. The words or phrases we adopt in our practices influence how we see students, how we respond to challenges, and how we show up in justice-centered work. When we are intentional about our language and align words with just actions, we can create purposeful environments and a culture that reinforces beliefs about equity.

Most teachers I work with through consulting experiences, graduate studies, and professional learning opportunities, continue to use equity terminology—*despite anti-DEI policies*—in their schools to guide their work with students. From my experience within educational contexts, equity does not have the negative meaning that conservative groups attribute to it. The term, equity, continues to live in conversations and the work of many teachers who care about the outcomes and well-being of all students. However, I recognize the fear that exists from real consequences of making equity visible in school publications, learning experiences, and institutional documents or webpages. If we cannot physically name 'equity' or terms without penalty, then our common language could be definitions rather than terms. *We use our power to create environments where all children thrive and commit to the removal of barriers that harm their access to resources, wellness, or academic achievement.* It is possible for equity to live in statements, practices, and learning experiences without being named, which will be further discussed in Chapter 7 when we explore ways to combat resistance.

A common language for DEI work not only defines terminology, but helps us to internalize expectations, reduce misunderstandings, and foster collaboration as people work from a shared purpose. For some DEI practitioners, building a common language may involve the work of helping educators to internalize established, institutional definitions of equity (or other justice-centered terminology) in personalized ways. For example, school districts may already have a working definition of inclusion, belonging, equity, or justice—*drafted by superintendents, school board members, and other stakeholders*—prior to the hiring of a DEI director. In this scenario, district leaders have likely identified disparities in data, developed a strategic action plan, and already have accountability systems in place. However, the understanding, definition, and associated goals of equity may not have transferred from the offices of district leaders or school board rooms into school buildings. This type of disconnect forces us to bridge communication and knowledge gaps, helping educators to understand the vision of a district and how educational equity is connected to their work with students.

Communication gaps are a common disconnect that I have witnessed in school districts via consulting work. Superintendents and directors believe that DEI work is happening based on their development of a strategic plan and commitment statements that are visible to the community. Meanwhile, teachers (and sometimes principals) may have no idea what is actually being done to achieve equity, nor understand all the components of strategic plans. This type of misalignment also causes confusion among community members who value DEI efforts. For example, I have worked with families who applauded a district's visible DEI stance yet felt like the efforts were not evident in their child's school. Therefore, the words from a school district become 'lip service' because the actual work does not live in schools.

If you work in a school district where working definitions of educational equity, racial justice, inclusion, or other DEI-related literacy exist and are publicized for community stakeholders and staff, please consider the following questions:

1 How is equity literacy defined in your school district (e.g., equity, belonging, justice, etc.)? Whose scholarship do the definitions stem from?
2 Are all employees familiar with the working definitions of equity literacy?
3 Can teachers and school staff identify where educational equity (or other justice-centered terminology) lives within their building and work with children?
4 Are teachers aware of district or school goals that discuss the advancement of equity?
5 What areas of a district's strategic plan align with school improvement goals?
6 Do educators understand their role in the creation of equitable environments in relation to the working definition of educational equity?
7 Can families identify the collective efforts among staff and school leadership to ensure inclusive and responsive environments for all students?

We can assess whether equity literacy has taken root within systems through meaningful conversations with stakeholders. When we engage with people who have experiences with educational systems, we gain a better understanding of what is working well and can identify areas of improvement. Through the creation of opportunities that invite diverse perspectives to share feedback, we can determine if our initiatives, communication, and vision are impactful in the advancement of DEI work. Ongoing dialogue with stakeholders ensures that school districts remain inclusive, responsive, and committed to DEI work.

In efforts to assess progress toward equitable practices, I have met with many parent-teacher organizations, student advocacy and affinity groups, principals, teachers, and staff teams to engage in conversations with the intent of critically examining systems. These listening tours offered clarity and evidence of whether the district's intentions aligned with impact. Through parents, caregivers, and other stakeholder groups, I learned about the wins within schools and gained knowledge of areas that required my attention (e.g., schools opting out of SEL instruction). The continuous flow of perspectives and insights helped staff within my division to make adjustments and decisions that intentionally reflected the needs of our school community.

The size of the group can also be a determining factor for how we structure outlets for feedback. It may not be manageable or feasible to gain feedback from a space that is hosting a large number of people. Sometimes, we may have to coordinate opportunities for informative feedback and invest time in thoughtful planning. The construction of smaller groups may be beneficial for listening tours in efforts to make people feel more comfortable to participate. In smaller settings, community and school stakeholders have more opportunity to elevate their voice, ask questions, address concerns, and have meaningful discussions. Small group dynamics also lead to better connections between participants, including relationships between DEI practitioners and staff or community members. People I never knew would address me publicly and cordially in different contexts after my interactions with them during a listening tour. The following process demonstrates steps for devising small, structured focus groups to gain insights about the progression of DEI work:

- **Identification:** Identify the stakeholder groups you would like to hear from, which could include students, parents or caregivers, teachers, counselors, principals, instructional assistants, etc. Select 10–20 people to be a part of a specific focus group that pertains to the articulation, clarity, and visibility of DEI work. Avoid groups larger than 20 people in order to maximize time for rich discussions. To ensure broader participation from a particular stakeholder group, you might organize several sessions that invite various perspectives. Keeping the timeframe to an hour or less is also feasible. This is an example statement that can be used for various stakeholder groups to explain the purpose of gathering feedback.

  In our school district, we believe that all students deserve safe, welcoming spaces that help them to thrive socially and academically. Our strategic plan emphasizes goals to achieve a high-performing, responsive, and inclusive school community. Students need rigorous coursework, systems of support, and high-quality educators to have positive outcomes in school. As a school district, we value your *partnership and feedback. In efforts to strengthen the alignment between our vision and practices, we desire to learn more about your lived experiences in our school community. It is important to understand the perceptions and interpretations of goals that exist in relation to the progress of our strategic plan. You have been selected to participate in a focus group that will take place on *insert date* at *insert time and place*. Please contact *insert DEI practitioner* with any questions regarding the focus group. If you are unable to attend, please let us know. We are willing to provide other accommodations to gain your feedback. If you lack interest in this initiative, you can also let us know. We appreciate your attention to this matter and hope to see you there.*

- **Accessibility and accommodations:** Consider the resources that may be needed to grant full participation (e.g., translation devices, translators, interpreters, etc.).
- **Environment for focus groups:** Make sure there is an adequate space to accommodate the size of the group. Position seating arrangements in a circular format to set the tone for personal dialogue. As a DEI practitioner, it may be helpful to have another person present (e.g., school or district secretary) who can record responses. Therefore, we can remain in the moment and be fully present as a facilitator. The sessions should also include protocols to guide the conversation, such as prohibiting individuals from saying disparaging or dehumanizing remarks.
- **Meeting:** Start with a welcome, brief introductions, and reiteration of the purpose of the meeting. Hand out copies of the school district's mission, strategic plan, core values, or statements that reflect the vision for DEI work. Invite participants to read the documents and instruct them to highlight words or phrases that resonate. After a few minutes, encourage participants to share what they highlighted. **Ask the following questions:**
  - Are the words you highlighted a reflection of actions that are experienced within our school district? If so, please share how the word or phrases are exemplified in schools? If not, please provide an example of what you are not seeing in schools despite our commitment to create responsive learning environments?
  - What questions do you have about the district's goals and strategies that are designed to support student outcomes?
  - Are you aware of the specific things you can do to support these efforts?

The responses from focus groups provide a general pulse of the clarity of DEI work within systems. If a working definition of educational equity exists and more than half of the participants knew nothing about it nor language of the strategic plan, then there is a breakdown in communication that needs to be addressed and a leadership issue. You may also receive feedback that teachers are aware of the messaging about equity, but have no idea what that means in terms of the practices that should be implemented in classrooms. I have also worked with principals who understood their role in supporting school improvement measures, yet struggled to build capacity and lead collective efforts among staff. The feedback from small, structured groups provides the insights that are needed to make thoughtful, strategic decisions for capacity-building within schools. Importantly, the feedback aids our work to generate a common language. Figure 5.4 demonstrates the leadership implications from stakeholder feedback.

There are other ways to assess feedback regarding educational systems, outside of the scope of focus groups. Although I have not seen great response rates from survey distributions (even with incentives), it can certainly be another method to assess progress toward equitable practices. Since I value the work of building relationships and listening to people's stories, I choose methods that involve human interactions and dialogue. There are times when stakeholders have reached out to share concerns via phone or have called to inquire about their involvement in focus groups (wanting to be involved based on a neighbor's experience), and I have encouraged those families to meet with me in person. I want people to know that they are a valued member of my community and that their voice as well as presence matters.

There are DEI practitioners who are hired into districts or schools that do not have a working definition of educational equity, a strategic plan, or professional learning experiences that focus on culturally responsive practices. Conversations about inequalities in education, institutionalized racism, and how to eradicate malpractices may not be normalized topics. When a foundation for justice-centered work is nonexistent, we may need to provide more context for the adoption of equity terminology through quantitative (e.g., achievement and behavioral outcomes, attendance records, etc.) and qualitative data (e.g., student narratives, community-based accounts, etc.). Dwayne Chism (2022) suggests that DEI practitioners can build a common language for equity and coherence through three questions (p. 23).

1 Why equity?
2 What is our responsibility?
3 What actions are needed?

Breaking Down Barriers to Build a Common Language for DEI		
Stakeholder Feedback	**Barrier to DEI Common Language**	**Leadership Actions**
"We never knew there was a strategic plan."	Lack of transparency	Identify the communication methods used in a school or district, such as newsletters, weekly phone calls, social media, and mailers. Clearly articulate the district or school's equity-focused strategic plan and mission across these platforms in concise, clear messages.
"The district proclaims to value inclusion, but we don't see that in our child's school." "It's performative work. The 'district' publicizes equity efforts that are not happening in my school."	Lack of alignment between language and the actual culture	DEI practitioners could follow up with the parent or caregiver and invite them to share their insights with the school principal. If a teacher has shared this feedback, the DEI practitioner can work with the principal to determine the best approach to build capacity among staff. This could look like coaching, where the DEI practitioner provides guidance to a principal. It could also be a reset initiative where a DEI practitioner partners with the school, provides education, and works with the principal in their efforts to build a culture where equity work is visible.
"I suggested creating an affinity space for Black teachers. My principal said that initiative would not promote inclusion. Meanwhile, I feel isolated in my department."	Lack of knowledge or mirror work	It is hard to have a common language if words are co-opted for different meanings. DEI practitioners need to understand what equity and inclusion means to leaders as they work to advance it in schools. Learning that sheds light on historical contexts and the need for affirming environments is a productive measure.

Figure 5.4 Breaking down barriers to build a common language for DEI.

It is important to give educators the time to grapple with the 'why equity' question before the discussion of actions and strategies. Consider the following steps while working with educational leaders. This exercise could also be implemented with teachers to build capacity of understanding in DEI work under the facilitation of a principal or instructional specialist:

1 **Review data.** Provide school and district-level data, including achievement, discipline, enrollment, participation in AP and honors courses, attendance, graduation, outcomes for multilingual learners, etc.
2 **Reflect on noticings.** Ask staff to reflect on data through the following prompts: *What do you notice? What do you wonder?* You could have people set up their thoughts in a T-chart as depicted in Figure 5.5.
3 **Highlight inequities.** Give people time to wrestle with their reflections. Ask them to highlight any inequalities upon their review of data.
4 **Unpack inequalities:** Ask people to consider the why behind inequalities. "Why is participation lacking from girls within STEM programming?" Encourage people to document their reflections.
5 **Systems work:** Discuss the importance of improving systems and how we are all responsible for creating structures in school that help all students to achieve and thrive. Systems are human-created, and we all hold the power to collectively change outcomes. Ask participants the following questions:
   - What does the data indicate about the function of systems within our school?
   - What parts within our system (e.g., curriculum, schedules, procedures, etc.) need to be addressed based on identified inequalities? Be specific about the parts that need to be addressed.
   - What are we currently doing as a collective to address the parts of systems that need improvement?
   - What support is needed in relation to the improvement of systems?

What do you notice?	What do you wonder?
Ex. I notice that more boys are participating in STEM programming.	I wonder why the STEM program is lacking participation from girls. I wonder if stereotypes and bias contribute to the widening of representation gaps. I wonder if STEM environments feel exclusive.

Figure 5.5 Reflection of noticings and wonderings.

This exercise launches educators into guided conversations about educational equity. These are conversations that are data-focused, inquiry-minded, and results-oriented. It also demonstrates how complex it can be to address issues that have been a historical stain on systems. For instance, I have led exercises that have prompted teachers to list the conditions needed for learning. When conditions are identified and we shift the conversation to ways we can systematically build them (conditions), the discussion often becomes more intense. It is easy for most of us to name flaws as humans, yet it can be harder to identify a process for change and an approach that benefits everyone within a school community. I think it is advantageous to walk teachers through these types of exercises to enhance their depth of knowledge in systems work. It helps educators to not only identify inequities but to also consider their power and role in dismantling them. Every decision has a domino effect, and technical solutions may not be the answer to every problem.

Equity audits, from consultants outside of an institution, can also provide insightful information that answers the "why equity" question. The results and feedback from audits can help DEI practitioners in their work of building a common language. Although we have the ability to conduct our own audits, focus groups, and structures for feedback, sometimes it is helpful to contract with a third-party organization or individual who has a strong level of expertise and no connection to a school district to ensure an unbiased approach. It can be beneficial to have other qualified individuals affirm our observations, recommendations, and assessments. This method would require funding and a thoughtful vetting process. We may also have to consider the language we use in contract proposals in relation to our political climate (Ex. Requesting for someone to support student achievement rather than naming DEI work or the need for a DEI consultant). Figure 5.6 helps us to avoid bad actors if we choose to explore the approval of consultants in our work to build capacity and a common language for DEI.

Although feedback is valuable, naming what is problematic within educational systems doesn't change them. Deliberate actions must be devised to address the roots of a problem. Sometimes, the initial action step is to hold a critical conversation with our colleagues, teams, or supervisors about the parts of systems that need to change. We may need to call out malpractices or hold others accountable if they are not working toward institutional goals. However, it is hard to hold people accountable if we are not in the practice of courageousness or fear the reactions of our advocacy. This prompts us to think about our role in creating a culture where critical conversations are normalized.

Normalizing Critical Conversations

Critical conversations are honest and intentional dialogues that center challenging or controversial topics, which may include identity (e.g., race, gender,

Criteria for DEI Consultants

When researching consultants and organizations that support DEI work, it is important to consider the following criteria to guide your steps toward proposals.

1. **Track record:** Look for a consultant or organization that has a clear track record of DEI work. Review testimonials, previous projects, and the frameworks or research that guide their DEI work.
2. **Mission-aligned:** Ensure that work of a consultant or organization is aligned with district goals.
3. **Intersectional work:** Confirm that the consultant or organization embraces intersectional work that addresses race, class, disabilities, gender, and other social identities. Hire people who can see complex issues through multiple perspectives.
4. **Systems work:** Assess the experience of a consultant or organization as related to transformational leadership. This includes having the capacity to conduct audits or assessments with the purpose of changing systems.
5. **Strategic approach:** Ensure that the consultant or organization has a strategic approach in navigating conflicts and facilitating learning experiences.

Figure 5.6 Criteria for hiring DEI consultants.

etc.), systems work, interpersonal relationships, or power in educational contexts. These conversations require vulnerability, courageousness, and a spirit of curiosity in efforts to improve systems, practices, policies, or connections. Change within systems starts with our voice. We actively disrupt inequities by naming what is harmful with a call to action. Critical conversations are a catalyst for problem-solving and collective work, empowering people to share ideas and opportunities for growth.

Through consulting work, I have learned that many educational leaders struggle with critical conversations and enacting systems of accountability. There is a legitimate fear of confrontation leading to grievances or resignations. *If I push too hard or provide constructive feedback, teachers will look for another job or leave the profession altogether.* These fears or desires to protect self or relationships may cause some leaders to avoid critical conversations altogether. Figure 5.7 demonstrates reflective questions that yield to the avoidance of critical conversations among school leaders. These questions have surfaced in my work with principals when discussing what holds us back from speaking our truth.

School leaders' reluctance to hold individuals accountable can adversely affect the overall culture of a school. When behaviors of resistance are normalized, it makes teachers who are committed to educational justice question

Questions that Signal the Hesitations of Critical Conversations Among School Leaders	
The following questions explore reflections from school principals while talking about the challenges of critical conversations. These questions are honest thoughts that may cause school leaders to pull back from the implementation of systems work. **Directions:** Set aside time for mirror work to review these questions and consider what may hold you back from leading courageously. After identifying your own areas of growth, talk with accountability partners for a shared learning experience and map out a plan to support your leadership.	
Area of concern	**Reflective question**
Teacher feedback	*How do I package constructive feedback in ways that lead to change and not resentment?*
Racial disparities	*How can I talk about race in a political climate that emphasizes merit over equity? How can I empower people to understand their role in eliminating disparities without being met with resistance or defensiveness?* **Principals of color:** *How can I facilitate conversations about race among white colleagues without them being resentful of the conversation or my identity as an administrator of color who is pushing for racial justice?*
District initiatives	*How do I address concerns regarding the initiatives of a district and its negative impact on my school considering its unique needs? How do I assert my suggestions to executive leadership without being penalized and viewed as a naysayer?*
Malpractices	*How do I address an educator who is not aligned with school initiatives and negatively influences a school's culture?*
Parent or caregiver relationships	*How do I hold critical conversations with parents or caregivers in ways that yield to a partnership and not tension?*

Figure 5.7 Questions that signal hesitations of critical conversations among school leaders.

their value or sense of belonging. Through equity audits, I have learned that a school leader's inaction in the disruption of malpractices or inequities can harm working conditions. Teachers who are mission-aligned may feel overlooked and steadily grow frustrations toward administration or colleagues who do not walk in institutional values. Educational leaders need to practice and develop critical conversation skills to cultivate a culture that empowers staff to hold each other accountable.

Scenario-based practice provides educational leaders with a structured way to process complex situations from educational contexts. It allows school leaders the opportunity to strengthen their emotional intelligence and decision-making. As DEI practitioners, we can create opportunities and time for school leaders to flex their critical conversation muscles. Group-based scenario practice enables school leaders to learn collaboratively and align their strategies. Through collective problem-solving, school leaders are also empowered to practice and normalize a common language for equity. The following scenario-based practice is one of many that I have used in consulting work. Take an intentional pause to read the situation, process your reactions, and consider how you would facilitate this exercise with school leaders:

> *You are a principal who is a part of an instructional meeting with a small group (5) of educators to discuss subgroup data. The team is identifying students who have not shown growth or proficiency within a math unit of study. Teacher A shares that some of her students' outcomes would be different if their parents were more involved and valued the education of their children.*
>
> *Teacher B tells the group that a parent regularly brings her son late to school, causing him to miss the first few minutes of math instruction. She asserts that the parent doesn't care about her son's math grade. Teacher C states that teachers cannot care more about students than their families. A sense of frustration is evident. The instructional coach is present and is struggling to steer the conversation in a positive direction. How do you enter this conversation and address the ideologies that emerged through the discussion?*

Mindful communication involves bringing awareness, curiosity, active listening, and thoughtful approaches to human interactions (Chapman, 2019). It is important to clarify what we hear in discussions, inviting mirror work in efforts to understand someone's statements or beliefs. In the example scenario, educators were frustrated by the lack of academic growth and resorted to deficit ideologies about children and their caregivers to justify poor outcomes. These situations require us to acknowledge human emotions while also naming beliefs that hinder learning experiences. In efforts to draw teachers to a mirror, we may ask the following questions in this scenario:

- *Could you help me understand the belief that parents do not care about their child's education?*
- *Has there been personal outreach to learn more about the barriers that may exist—particularly, for students in the classroom—as related to achievement?*
- *How can we come alongside families and partner with them?*

The deficit ideology could also be directly addressed: *There were a few assumptions made about parents and their investment in educational outcomes for children. These assumptions come from underlying beliefs we need to process.* Educators need spaces where they can grapple with their beliefs, power, and actions. Scenario-based practice can help school leaders and teachers to learn more about their communication (e.g., tone, delivery, etc.), emotions, and impact while engaging in critical conversations.

We must also be realistic and prepare educators for pushback while navigating critical conversations. While working with individuals from different backgrounds, beliefs, and lived experiences, we cannot enter a conversation with the expectation that people will align with our perspectives or value our feedback. Additionally, if our approach to critical conversations reflects a commitment to curiosity, we must acknowledge the possibility that we may have limited context and need additional information. When engaging in scenario-based practices, I do ask educators to consider points of pushback and to devise clarifying questions. We should approach conversations with an open mind and proactively prepare for potential conflicts.

Many of us have worked in school districts where situations arose or poor decisions were made, but we may have been afraid to speak our truth. In some circumstances, the fear could not be discounted because people in positions of power made the reservations of educational staff valid. *I disagreed with the directive and offered another perspective, and now I'm being penalized for being honest.* We know there are educational leaders who use fear as a tool of compliance. A culture of fear promotes silence and compels people to protect the status quo rather than doing what is just. We cannot change systems if operating in spaces where fear diminishes our power.

The following steps are considerations for critical conversations. I advise DEI practitioners to get into the practice of speaking courageously prior to growing leaders. It is challenging to teach others a skill that we do not model in our professional or everyday lives. These steps help us to consider our awareness and approach to critical conversations.

Prior to Conversation (if pre-arranged):

- **Reflect on the purpose of the conversation.** Think about your beliefs and convictions as related to the topic. Do you understand the context surrounding the topic? Consider talking with an accountability partner to process your thoughts.
- **Think about your talking points and what needs to be raised in the conversation.** We do not need to look in a literal mirror and rehearse our talking points, yet we do need to consider the thoughts we want

to uplift in a conversation. Rehearsing can yield to an inorganic conversation where we are more focused on memorizing points than hearing another person's perspective. Process the articulation of your thoughts, while keeping a spirit of curiosity in mind.
- **Consider the outcomes of the conversation.** Reflect on the goals for the conversation. What is the desired outcome? (Internally note that some conversations will need revisiting, and others may not yield a positive outcome.)
- **Check your emotions and assess the situation.** Consider how you feel and do your own mirror work to determine any biases or assumptions that might be surfacing within your approach. Think about the best timing for the conversation.

Entering the Conversation:

- **Arrive with a spirit of curiosity.** Remember, we may have limited context and need additional information to process our thoughts, beliefs, and approaches.
- **Thank the participant(s) for their presence.** Demonstrate gratitude, recognizing the humanity and emotions that are within the room.
- **Breathe and embrace discomfort.** It is not supposed to feel good to elevate hard things.
- **Speak your truth.** Share your thoughts with an open mind, remaining conscious of your emotions, delivery, and impact (read the room).

During Conversation:

- **Actively listen to the response of the participant(s).** Listen for things that are said and unsaid. Raise clarifying questions to understand what a person is trying to convey, using their words. Try to understand the root of the issue.
- **Work collectively to determine a problem-solving process.** If possible, try to co-construct solutions with participant(s). *What can we do to change this issue? What support is needed?*

Figure 5.8 provides sentence-starters for critical conversations. As a former kindergarten teacher, I spent most instructional days building social and advocacy skills among young learners. I often taught children "I" statements to empower them to use their voice. Whether on the playground or in the classroom, students confidently expressed their feelings and needs. *I did not*

Ways to Approach a Critical Conversation
Using "I" statements

- I noticed (insert what happened), and I wondered your thoughts regarding the matter.
- I would like to connect and chat about something that I have been thinking about.
- I need to collaborate with you and discuss a situation that needs problem-solving. When can we connect?
- I think we are processing this situation differently, and I would like to hear your perspective.
- I sense that something feels off between us. Could we talk about it? I value our relationship.
- I heard what you said during (insert meeting) and wanted to revisit the statement. Could you help me understand the context surrounding the statement? What did you mean by that statement?

Figure 5.8 Ways to approach a critical conversation.

like it when you pushed me down the slide. However, as adults, many of us struggle to use "I" statements and refrain from sharing our internal thoughts. We need to lead with courage and model mindful communication. Our voice is a powerful tool and pathway for changing systems and outcomes of students.

Building a culture of belonging, inclusion, and justice means that we cultivate environments where critical conversations live. Without honest dialogue, unjust and exclusionary practices persist. When we build a common language for equity, we not only develop meaningful language to describe our work but also create a guide for human interactions and practices. Building from the development of an inclusive culture, Chapter 6 will talk more about the protection of civil and human rights. Students and educational staff deserve environments that are free of harassment and discrimination. We can foster work and learning environments where people feel safe to participate, contribute ideas, and be their authentic selves.

Chapter Highlights

1 Mirror and shadow work helps us to remain connected to our humanity. We need to intentionally engage in introspective practices that foster growth in leadership and human development.
2 Systems work encourages us to understand what creates, perpetuates, and sustains educational inequities. The work of

transforming systems also compels us to think about how we build capacity for equitable practices, including strategies for building a common language—*words, actions and shared beliefs*—that promotes equity.

3 Critical conversations are necessary for the disruption and transformation of unjust systems. We need to model courageousness in our human interactions and foster a culture where vulnerable, honest conversations about educational systems and outcomes are normalized.

Mirror Work

1 Review Figure 5.2 and other reflective questions from this chapter that ask you to think about your leadership identity. Consider what you have learned about your leadership. Describe the leader you aspire to be.

References

Adams, M. (2022). *Change your questions, change your life: 12 powerful tools for leadership, coaching, and results*. Inquiry Institute Library Series. Berrett-Koehler Publishers.

Chapman, S. (2019). *How mindful communication makes us more compassionate*. Mindful. https://www.mindful.org/stop-go-wait/

Chism, D. (2022). *Leading your school toward equity: A practical framework for walking the talk*. ASCD.

Freire, P. (2022). *Pedagogy of the oppressed* (50th anniversary edition). Bloomsbury Academic Publishing.

Gruenert, G., & Whitaker, T. (2015). *School culture rewired: How to define, assess, and transform it*. 1st ed. ASCD.

hooks, b. (2001). *All about love: New visions*. Harpers Collins.

Jung, C. G. (1979). *Anion: Researchers into the phenomenology of self*. (Collected Works of C.G. Jung Vol. 9 Part 2). Princeton University Press.

Kafele, B. (2018). *Is my school a better school because I lead it?* ASCD.

Muhammad, A. (2018). *Transforming school culture: How to overcome staff division. 2nd ed.* Solution Tree Press.

6

Showing Up for Human and Civil Rights

Exploring Title IX, Title VI, and the ADA

Human rights are basic freedoms and safeguards that belong to every individual. As humans, we have the right to live full lives where we can be our authentic selves. Civil rights include protections from inhumane treatment, including all forms of violence, harassment, and discrimination based on race, gender, class, religion, or other statuses. No matter the context, each person has a right to justice and environments that ensure psychological and physical safety.

Justice-centered work in schools ensures that everyone is treated with human dignity. It includes efforts to create equal opportunities, fair policies or practices, and an inclusive culture. Students, families, and educational staff deserve environments that are supportive, anti-oppressive, and free from harassment or discrimination. While DEI practitioners are positioned to foster inclusionary work, some take on the additional responsibilities of enacting and overseeing policies to comply with civil rights laws. We may need to develop procedures, professional learning, and documentation tools for legal assurances to abide by policies such as Title IX, Title VI, or the Americans with Disabilities Act (ADA) and/or state-equivalent laws.

As a DEI practitioner, I served as the Title IX and Title VI coordinator, with duties varying by district. I managed instructional systems, coordinated professional development and student programs, and created procedures for addressing and investigating discrimination complaints. There were times when I had to abruptly pivot from tasks or a professional learning experience to address allegations of sexual assault or harassment. Middle schoolers with

DOI: 10.4324/9781032623542-6

cell phones often kept me busy—*to extreme levels of exhaustion*—as a result of them using their devices as a vehicle to either harass peers or engage in unwanted sexting. Most investigations were time-consuming, particularly if attorneys or media were involved. Those challenges taught me the importance of proactive work to combat to acts of discrimination.

If your job involves handling claims of harassment and discrimination, this chapter will discuss important factors to consider for effective policy implementation. DEI practitioners who are not directly involved in these aspects of legal compliance are encouraged to review this chapter and utilize relevant information as needed. If materials concerning sexual harassment or assault cause distress, it is recommended to refrain from engaging with the Title IX section unless you are serving as a designated coordinator. Despite variances in job descriptions, we all hold a legal obligation to ensure safe working and learning environments that are free of sexism, racism, ableism, and other forms of discrimination.

Understanding Title IX: Policy Implementation for DEI Practitioners

Although the Civil Rights Act of 1964 prohibited discrimination based on race, color, religion, sex, or national origin, there was no legal framework to address sexism or to ensure gender equality in institutions. Women lacked access to opportunities, facilities, and scholarships in sports. At all levels of education, girls and women encountered circumstances of sexual harassment or assault. Title IX of the Education Amendments of 1972 was developed to prohibit discrimination based on sex (Boschert, 2022). It is a civil rights law that applies to schools and any educational program that operates with federal financial assistance.

The Department of Education's Office for Civil Rights (OCR) has historically enforced Title IX in educational facilities to ensure non-discriminatory environments. OCR provides non-binding legal guidance to schools to help educational leaders remain in compliance with Title IX. The OCR conducts investigations and assesses whether alleged complaints meet the definition of discrimination or harassment. For conduct to meet the legal definition of 'sexual harassment,' it must be found severe, pervasive, and objectively offensive enough that it essentially prevents someone from having equal access to an educational program or activity. This includes adversely impacting one's educational experience or hindering participation in opportunities offered by the institution. If school administrators do not uphold Title IX requirements or violate policies, the Office for Civil Rights (OCR) may require corrective actions to improve compliance systems, with noncompliance potentially resulting in the withdrawal of federal funding. Think of it as a never-ending checklist that concludes only when the OCR determines your district has made progress to show compliance.

Title IX has been marked with significant shifts in policies, interpretations, and enforcement with each presidential term over time. Under the Biden administration, there were broader definitions of sex, inclusive of gender identity and sexual orientation, and differences in the Title IX complaint process. While writing this book in between two different presidential administrations in the United States, the pendulum has already swung back to the exclusion of people who identify as transgender. The OCR's enforcement of Title IX "depends on the willingness of the political party in charge of the executive branch and on the federal resources allocated to the agency" (Boschert, 2022, p. 272). Defunding the Department of Education also means a destabilization of resources distributed to the OCR. It is important to stay abreast of this evolving area of law and to lean on the wisdom of legal experts, which I did for this chapter.

Although Title IX regulations continuously change, the proactive work of creating inclusive environments that are free of harassment and discrimination remains the same. Sexual misconduct accounted for 29% of Title IX violations reported in fiscal year 2019 (Boschert, 2022). It is necessary to change the conditions that yield to sex discrimination and develop systems of accountability (Boschert, 2022). For DEI practitioners who are deemed as Title IX coordinators, there are several action steps needed to protect the human and civil rights of students and educational staff within schools:

1 Establish or ensure that your school district has an updated non-discrimination/anti-harassment policy.
2 Determine procedures to enact the anti-harassment/non-discrimination policy, including systems for reporting and actions to prevent retaliation.
3 Designate school-based coordinators or designees to work in conjunction with the District Title IX Coordinator.
4 Ensure that procedures for reporting are visible and known to staff, students, and community stakeholders.
5 Provide education to students, educational staff, and families that addresses the following: (a) the definition of harassment; (b) behaviors that constitute harassment; (c) signs of harassment and what to look for if you suspect someone is being harassed; and (d) what you can do if you or someone else is experiencing sexual harassment.

6 Develop systems of support to ensure that complainants and respondents have resources and assistance.
7 Periodically conduct a needs-assessment among students and educational staff to determine areas of growth to improve systems.

Non-Discrimination and Title IX Policies

A non-discrimination policy is a set of guiding principles that ensures fairness, safety, and equality within a workplace. It provides clarity of practices and the behaviors all members should adopt within a school community. Title IX mandates certain elements in a school's non-discrimination policy, but school districts may vary in how they implement and supplement those requirements (Heiser, 2025). An effective non-discrimination policy will apply to all areas or services of an organization and should describe a district's commitment to provide safe environments. It will also include a list of protected classes or groups of people who are legally safeguarded from discrimination under federal, state, or local laws. Although protected classes can change based on a political party's actions under the executive branch, it is important to note that a school board can adopt a policy that protects classes regardless of changes in the executive branch's interpretation of the laws (Heiser, 2025). The following is an example statement of language from a non-discrimination student policy:

> ***[Insert School]*** *will not discriminate on the basis of race, color, national or ethnic origin, religion, gender, disability, or sexual orientation in administration of its educational program, policies, athletics, or extracurricular activities.*

A Title IX policy will specify that sex-based discrimination is prohibited in any school or educational program that receives funding. It should promote gender equality, ensuring that all genders have equal access to resources, opportunities, and programs in education. Additionally, Title IX policies should convey that a school district will protect students and educational staff against all forms of sexual discrimination, harassment, and assault. The policy should define sex-based discrimination (with reference to current laws), list procedures for reporting complaints of harassment, and describe the investigation process. Generally, Title IX policies within school districts prohibit the following actions:

- Sexual assault
- Uninvited sexual advances or requests for sexual favors
- Stalking

- Spreading rumors of sexual activity
- Commenting about an individual's body or sexual experiences
- Sexually suggestive touching, comments, or gestures in interpersonal relationships
- Sex-stereotyping or pressuring someone to conform to a sex-based stereotype

Non-discrimination policies, including Title IX, are established to ensure that the actions of students and educational staff align with legal obligations as well as a district's commitment to create safe environments. The policies serve as a framework that guides behaviors and decisions within a school community. Title IX policies should clearly specify accountability measures, outlining how rules are enforced, integrated in workplace culture, and addressed if violated. Policy work in general should involve the leadership of superintendents, school board members, and school district attorneys.

DEI practitioners serving as District Title IX Coordinators should work collaboratively with executive leaders who are responsible for policy development. We should feel empowered to offer feedback or revisions to Title IX policies, ensuring that recommendations are supported by relevant laws and legal counsel. For example, in my first DEI role I worked with the school board to guide their decision-making in the adoption of a non-discrimination policy. There were several members of the school board who did not feel inclined to include protected classes in the policy, questioning the role of race and gender. The tension within the decision-making process led to a work board session where I prepared an educational presentation to discuss why vulnerable communities needed protections. This session was memorable because I spent over an hour defending my own humanity while advocating for students from minoritized groups. Sometimes we must do the unfortunate work of enlightening people in positions of power- *who may be certified bigots-* to advocate for the needs of students and staff.

Guidelines and Procedures for Title IX Policies

Students and educational staff need to know the contact information of the District Title IX Coordinator and the individuals who are designated in their schools or departments to receive complaints of harassment. The guidelines should incorporate information about the complaint process, including how a person can file a complaint and the documentation that is required. Whether submissions are collected through a form, an electronic portal, or anonymous reporting systems, the information should go directly to Title

IX coordinators (district or school level) and designated staff (e.g., superintendents, safety/security departments, school-based law enforcement, etc.). Students and educational staff need access to a reporting system where they can describe incidents of discrimination or harassment. The information should be acquired by a Title IX coordinator who can promptly launch an investigation. The following information should be included in an electronic complaint form:

- Name of reporting party
- Grade level, position, or affiliation of reporting party
- Phone number
- Email address
- Physical address
- Date of incident
- Time of incident
- Location of incident
- Indication of involvement (Ex. Did the individual witness the incident or receive information from another party? This could be organized in a multiple-choice format.)
- Description of incident
- People involved

The timeline of the investigation process should also be outlined in the procedures. Attorneys who specialize in school law and partner with districts should be able to define timelines and processes for resolving complaints in accordance with laws. For instance, as a coordinator in my first DEI role, I worked under Title IX guidelines that conveyed that the school district had 60 days to complete an investigation, present findings, and develop a resolution for all parties involved. Although it is important to act swiftly upon the receipt of a complaint, it can be helpful to have a timeline that allows you to have a comprehensive and thorough investigation. As someone who has investigated Title IX complaints involving athletic teams and student clubs, it is helpful to have extended time when situations require interviews with multiple students and families.

All members of a school community should know their Title IX coordinators, how to file a complaint, and the timelines and action steps associated with the investigation process. The guidelines should convey how individuals involved in investigations will be protected, offering assurances of confidentiality whenever legally permissible. Additionally, students and educational staff should know how members in a school district will be held accountable for their actions if harassment is substantiated, retaliation is enacted, or confidentiality is broken. The timeline for an investigation may vary, but typically a formal complaint process involves these steps:

1. A formal complaint is submitted by the reporting party or initiated by the District Title IX Coordinator to jumpstart the investigation process.
2. All parties involved should receive a notice of allegations, abiding by the timeline designated in the Title IX policy.
3. An investigation is conducted where all parties are interviewed. Please note that parents or caregivers may want to be present during interviews, which is their right when situations involve minors. Some school districts may contract with a third-party investigator or a reviewer of evidence to eliminate bias and conflicts of interest. (Note: For circumstances that involve multiple people, I highly recommend seeking a third-party investigator and wish I would have known that pro-tip earlier as a District Title IX Coordinator.)
4. Evidence related to allegations of harassment or discrimination is collected from interviews and all parties involved.
5. All parties are provided time to review evidence and have a period of time to respond to the documentation that has been collected by the District Title IX Coordinator.
6. An investigative report is drafted (by either the District Title IX Coordinator or third-party investigator) and reviewed by a school district attorney. The report is sent to all parties for their review of findings.

School-Based Title IX Coordinators

District Title IX Coordinators do not have the bandwidth to investigate multiple claims simultaneously, in addition to carrying out responsibilities that do not involve the elimination of harassment. To build capacity, it is helpful to designate a Title IX coordinator or designee at each school who can receive claims, lead investigations, and share findings with the District Title IX Coordinator (responsible for formal complaint process). School-based Title IX coordinators should receive ongoing training that centers policy language, procedures, and the investigation process. Oftentimes, I would invite attorneys to conduct sessions and scenario-based practices with school-level coordinators. School-based coordinators need dedicated time and space to ask questions, collaborate, and share resources.

In my experience, most school-based Title IX coordinators or designees were building administrators, and some were social workers or counselors. As a pro-tip, I would advocate for an administrator (e.g., assistant principal, dean, etc.) to be a school-based Title IX coordinator in efforts to allow social workers or counselors to be in a role where they can solely offer support to students. It is challenging to be an investigator and a key staff member who delivers emotional support for all parties involved. School-based Title IX coordinators should work closely with the District Title IX Coordinator, keeping them abreast of all investigations and claims.

School-based Title IX coordinators should learn documentation techniques for investigations and discuss strategies to protect alleged victims. When students or staff report harassment, it is necessary to accurately document what is shared through interviews and noted through body language (e.g., noting the dispositions of those involved). Importantly, school-based Title IX coordinators should orchestrate systems of support for all parties involved while investigating claims. As mentioned, I prefer school-based Title IX coordinators to be administrators so counselors, social workers, or mental health providers can be responsive to emotional needs. Support during an active investigation may also look like the provision of accommodations. Students may require schedule adjustments or route changes to avoid certain classmates, as well as 'no contact orders' to restrict communication or interaction between specific individuals. In more serious situations, law enforcement might intervene by issuing protective orders that prevent contact or interactions between those involved in the investigation. Teachers and educational staff may need to work with Human Resources (HR) to determine appropriate safeguards if experiencing harassment from a colleague or staff member. Figure 6.1 is an example of a template that school-based Title IX coordinators could use to record incidents and findings of an investigation. In my experiences, these documents were forms that were constantly shared with school

Date of Incident	School/ Location	Parties Involved (add student IDs)	Lead Investigator	Brief Description of Incident	Safeguards for Parties Involved	Pending or Closed Investigation (Describe outcomes)
5/25/26	Madison Elementary	James Pitts and Emily Rose	Buchanan-Rivera	Unwanted physical touch (**Note**: *A thorough description or report could be linked here too*).	'No contact' orders in place for students.	Pending

Figure 6.1 Title IX incident tracker.

attorneys to (a) keep attorneys abreast of developing cases and (b) protect the information through attorney-client privileges.

Visibility of Procedures and Title IX Policy Language

While working in a school district that was reported to the Office for Civil Rights (OCR), one of the OCR's recommendations was to make the Title IX policy, reporting process, and contact information of coordinators accessible for all stakeholders. (Note: *Contact info may be listed in the policy or reporting process.*) Most districts have policy documents and electronic reporting tools on their websites, but sometimes these resources are difficult for community members to locate. Take the time to assess the accessibility of your own district's reporting system or policies. If your school's Title IX policy or reporting process isn't readily visible, it's likely buried under multiple links and not easily accessible.

As a DEI practitioner, I have encountered cases involving teachers or administrators accused of sexual misconduct with students or staff. When these situations emerge and make headlines, it significantly impacts a school's culture. If institutional commitments to safety have been broken, healing begins by listening to those who feel harmed. By collaborating with students in advocacy clubs, I have learned that information about Title IX procedures should be accessible in the places where students congregate. Oftentimes, students will hear or see something pertaining to a discriminatory act, prior to educational staff. We need students to be a part of the proactive work of eliminating harassment and discrimination, which means they need to have knowledge of reporting systems and quick access to Title IX information.

Policy language can be visible through student handbooks or flyers on campus with QR codes that link to reporting systems. Furthermore, details regarding reporting procedures should be prominently displayed in restrooms, classrooms, cafeterias, libraries, hallways, and other areas where students frequently meet. I have also made student videos for televised announcements that have addressed concepts, such as sexting and digital footprints. We need to make the legal language of policies relevant and visible for students so they understand Title IX, actions needed for safe environments, and how violations could potentially impact their future selves.

Education of Title IX Policies, Guidelines, and Procedures

Not only do Title IX coordinators need ongoing training, but educational staff, students, and families need education about policy language and procedures too. To reiterate, education should include (a) the definition of harassment, (b) behaviors that constitute harassment, (c) signs of harassment, and (d) actions to take if experiencing harassment. Many school districts have training videos at the start of a school year that are frankly box checkers for compliance. Let's be honest, I am not the only person who has played videos in the background while doing several pressing things. Therefore, I suggest a humanizing approach to education where Title IX coordinators or district administrators directly engage with staff to clarify information and procedures. For example, I have coordinated sessions where attorneys have educated staff on the protections and rights of students who identify as transgender and non-binary. Considering the rise of anti-LGBTQ+ laws in multiple states, it was important to create learning opportunities where educators could unpack policies and the impact of legislation on classrooms. It helps to provide time for shared learning where staff can wrestle with real-time issues, collaborate, and ask questions in environments that promote an open dialogue.

Students also need education about harassment and discrimination. While writing this chapter, I watched the four-part Netflix series called Adolescence. (Spoiler Alert) It features the arrest of a 13-year-old boy, Jamie Miller, who murdered a girl named Katie Leonard, who was his classmate. As the investigation and Jamie's therapy sessions unfold during his incarceration, we learn more about the way subcultures, social media, and toxic masculinity influence the behaviors and ideologies of young men. The film reminded me of several Title IX investigations where students believed their actions of sexual misconduct were justified and 'normalized' in teen culture. For example, I have read student text messages as a part of Title IX investigations that have included vulgar, sexual language. In those situations, I have been told directly by male students that sexual language is a normalcy among teens and "what girls want to hear." Furthermore, teenage girls have shared the same sentiments and expressed that they did not disrupt inappropriate texts or jokes because "that's just how guys talk!"

I have also worked through sexual assault cases involving students, including many from LGBTQ+ communities. Since most schools do not implement inclusive sex education, some students feel compelled to explore their sexual identities through the use of pornography, which does not often show caring, loving sexual relationships (Richards, 2020). Some students unfortunately act out inappropriate learned behaviors, which yields to traumatic experiences for all parties involved. The access that students have to harmful ideologies and misconceptions of sexual or romantic relationships is startling, which calls for more education that addresses belief systems and societal influences in teen culture.

Educational opportunities for students and staff should not only outline procedures for reporting but should also shed light on signs of harassment. We know that fear, shame, and loss of opportunities can hold people back from reporting an incident. I personally understand the costs that come with speaking your truth and recognize the lengths people will go to protect themselves or an institution. We need to disrupt harm and advocate for others who are on the receiving end of discriminatory practices. If someone is experiencing harassment, the following signs may be evident:

- depression and anxiety
- feelings of blame, guilt, and shame
- physical illness
- increased absenteeism
- poor performance

In the book, Just Mercy, Bryan Stevenson wrote that "If we recognize the signs, we are all implicated when we allow other people to be mistreated" (2018, p. 18). When we see signs of harassment or discrimination, we need to say something. Recognizing harassment and remaining silent, breeds more harm. We need staff members to identify traits of harassment and report their observations to school-based Title IX coordinators who can initiate an investigation. School systems can be set up to respond appropriately when information is promptly reported.

Understanding Title VI

Some DEI practitioners are also Title VI coordinators. Title VI was also passed as a part of the Civil Rights Act of 1964 and prohibits discrimination based on race, color, or national origin in programs and institutions that receive federal funding (Urban & Wagoner, 2014). This means that students and educational staff should not be denied opportunities or excluded from experiences based on race or ethnicity. DEI practitioners who serve as Title VI coordinators not only have to enact actions aligned with non-discrimination policies (similar to the steps outlined in the Title IX section) but must also focus on antiracism and the development of racially affirming environments. Therefore, this section will address practical strategies and the ideological work that is needed to uproot racism from policies, practices, and school systems. It is important to have robust policies and systems for reporting racial discrimination, but it is equally essential to focus on the dismantlement of racist ideologies to ensure lasting change.

Addressing Institutional Racism and Identity Threats

When people think about racism, images of violence, racial slurs, and hate-driven groups may emerge. However, there are more subtle forms of racism

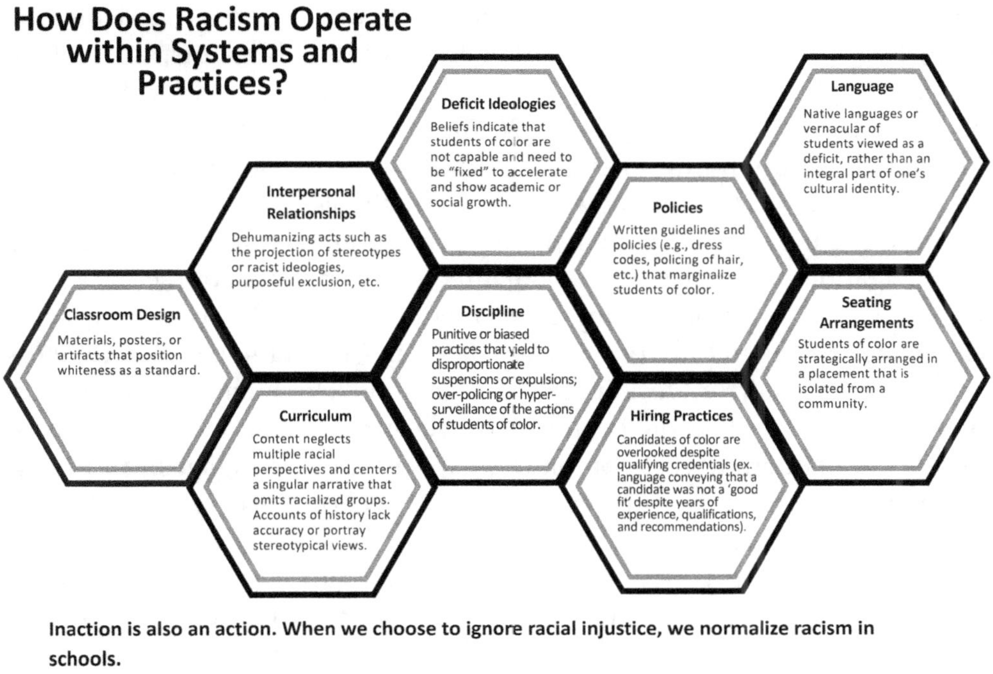

Figure 6.2 How does racism operate within systems and practices.

that are widespread and deeply rooted in societal systems (see Figure 6.2). As a Black student, there were moments when I experienced explicit forms of racism through dehumanizing language. Racism was also visible through actions that perpetuated the erasure of my identity. My childhood experiences reflected white educators who often highlighted white authors, stories, guest speakers, and contextual examples that did not mirror my racial identity or history. It sent a strong message that whiteness was the standard that should be acknowledged and celebrated, which became a catalyst for my advocacy, research, and first book. Racism is a system of oppression that rests on the premise that one race is superior to others. It can thrive within the ideologies that are used to create systems, policies, and practices at an institutional level.

Undoing racism in school environments requires the work of fostering race-conscious educators, staff, and students. Contrary to the beliefs of numerous politicians and oppositional groups, children need to learn about racism and how to respond to racial injustice. Research indicates that children who learn about racism and racial differences tend to value diversity and are better able to identify discrimination when it happens (Apfelbaum et al., 2010). As practitioners, we need to understand how whiteness operates and influences practices, and learn how to talk about race in ways that promote inclusion, upstanders, and just systems. Numerous scholars of anti-racist work uplift that people of all shades can uphold and act on racist ideologies. For instance, if an educator has absorbed the belief that Black men are violent, they would likely expect or look for criminal behavior from Black boys as indicative of the Yale Study (Bender, 2016) mentioned in Chapter 2. When we intentionally study how whiteness breathes within our own living systems, we can begin to understand how it infiltrates schools.

Racism is the interlocking thread that impacts all identities and influences our navigation in life. If we can dismantle the strongholds of racism within schools, we can eliminate many other identity threats that plague systems (Combahee River Collective, 1977). As stated in Chapter 4, DEI practitioners can incorporate mirror work into professional development to prompt educators and staff to reflect on the impact of racism in schools and personal contexts. Without internal work, it is hard to expect people to engage in anti-racist leadership where they normalize conversations about race, identify disparities, and advocate for systemic changes that promote racial equity. Figure 6.3 demonstrates mirror work questions that support the development of a racial consciousness. Some of the questions can also be found in *Identity Affirming Classrooms: Spaces that Center Humanity* (Buchanan-Rivera, 2022, p. 22).

It takes a comprehensive approach to advance racial equity in schools. Educational staff not only need opportunities for introspective work but also need time to grapple with culturally responsive practices. As mentioned in Chapter 4, professional learning communities can be a time for teachers to strengthen their collective impact and discuss strategies to eliminate racial disparities. Building capacity also involves the work of creating a common language for racial equity, developing learning experiences, and empowering

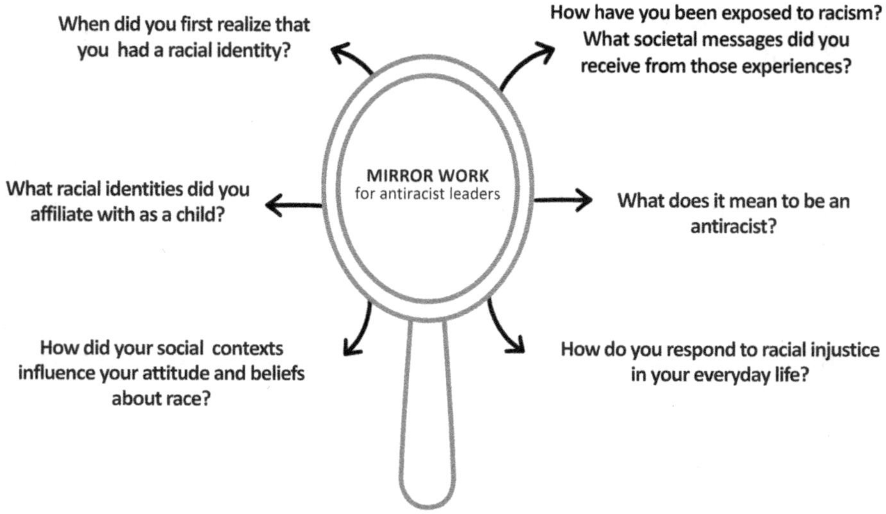

Figure 6.3 Mirror work for anti-racist leaders.

students and staff to challenge racist ideologies and discriminatory behaviors. Everyone within a school setting should feel compelled to dismantle institutional racism and advocate for policy changes to promote racial justice. We are all responsible for eliminating racism in classrooms and within educational systems. The following action steps are things we can do as DEI practitioners to enact Title VI policies and promote antiracism in schools:

1 **Policy alignment:** Ensure that non-discrimination policies are in alignment with language from Title VI and organizational objectives to ensure safe environments. The policy should define actions that constitute as racial discrimination. Similar to Title IX, guidelines, procedures, and systems of accountability should be outlined within policies to help people understand the reporting and investigation process for racial discrimination claims.
2 **Approach and competence:** As a DEI practitioner, consider your approach for leading and facilitating anti-racist work. Are you knowledgeable of historical contexts or grounded in scholarship? Do you facilitate discussions in a way that promotes engagement and reflection? Do you have a plan in mind in the event someone attempts to hijack your talking points? Competence is critical when engaging in topics that are perceived as 'controversial' and people will challenge you. Base your work on academic research, experience, and data. There is no need to argue with anyone when you have facts and receipts. The following questions, often presented in a contentious manner, are what I refer to as the "greatest hits of racial equity PDs." I can guarantee that a variation of these questions will be raised, especially when facilitating as a Black woman in a predominately white space.
   - Why are we focusing on race instead of merit? My life was full of challenges, and I worked hard to be successful.
   - When you state that students need to see themselves reflected in teachers and leaders in schools, are you saying that white people can't teach or supervise students of color?
   - How is this training unifying us? It feels like it is causing more division.
   - White people are not solely responsible for harming marginalized communities. What about Black-on-Black crime?
   - What is the point of this history other than to make us feel guilt? We are not responsible for our ancestors.

   Be informed and anticipate resistance, as some may view the acknowledgment of racial disparities as divisive. I have purposefully collected challenging questions (the greatest hits) over the years to practice and prepare for controversial moments.

3 **Build capacity:** Work closely with school leaders, particularly principals, to build capacity for anti-racist education. School leaders need opportunities to examine their understanding of racism, recognizing that it extends beyond one's prejudice and infiltrates policies, practices, and systems. Principals set the tone for a school's culture and need to model anti-racist leadership with competence. The practice of naming racial inequities, disrupting racism, and having critical conversations should be ongoing learning for school leaders. (Pro-tip: Provide time for principals to engage with the questions from Figure 6.3).

4 **Create learning opportunities:** Develop a system for continuous professional learning that provides educators the opportunity to engage in mirror work and anti-racist pedagogies. Educators need to understand the formation of their own racial identity and how race influences interactions, practices, and their navigation within the world. We need to learn about concepts such as curriculum violence (Ighodaro & Wiggan, 2013; Jones, 2020), civic discourse, and culturally responsive teaching that is grounded in scholarship. Revisit, Books for Professional Growth and Human Development (Figure 4.9).

5 **Partner with curricular teams:** Collaborate with curriculum departments to assess texts, programs, and instructional materials, ensuring students have access to resources and opportunities that showcase diverse representation and affirm their communities. Remember, it is not enough to have a diverse representation of books on a shelf. Teachers need to know how to use texts and instructional materials to have critical conversations that foster human development.

6 **Form equity teams at both school and district levels:** Establish equity teams to build capacity and promote a shared understanding of racial literacy within schools (refer to Chapter 4). These teams are responsible for identifying, discussing, and addressing racial disparities as reflected in achievement, programming, and climate data. They should communicate outcomes, strategies, and action steps to staff in alignment with district goals. Equity teams can also offer valuable professional learning opportunities that help educators strengthen their ability to implement culturally responsive teaching in classrooms.

7 **Develop affinity spaces:** Consider the development of racial affinity spaces for educational staff and students. Affinity groups are

communities formed by people with shared identities, experiences, or interests. These groups offer support, empowerment, and spaces for healing, especially within unjust systems (see Chapter 7). Affinity groups require strong facilitation to ensure a purposeful space. The Interaction Institute for Social Change offers a Racial Affinity Group Field Guide, which provides more context on the organization and facilitation of these healing spaces (Note: The field guide is listed in the references of this chapter as Interactive Institute for Social Change, 2025).

8 **Assess needs:** Develop a needs assessment or racialized focus groups to assess progress toward racial equity. Through equity audits, I have facilitated community and institutional focus groups that have centered the voices of people of color. The information that is collected from these sessions can be used as a measuring stick to determine a school district's commitment to racial justice and alignment to Title VI.

For DEI practitioners who identify as Black, Indigenous, or a person of color, the work of disrupting racism can be emotionally taxing. It is hard to be in a position where you constantly feel as if you have to defend your existence. As a Black educator and parent, this work is personal and impacts my everyday life. It is difficult to process the glaring racial disparities that exist within schools, as well as my own survival stories within educational systems. Racial segregation in schools was outlawed over 70 years ago, since the *Brown v. Board* (1954) ruling and Canada closed its last racially segregated school in Ontario over 60 years ago (Henry-Dixon, 2021). Despite the time that has passed from desegregation mandates across the globe, we know that many educators are still grappling with culturally responsive practices and how to meet the needs of students of color. And, if we could have an honest moment… It is even more frustrating to know that many fellow colleagues in education align with the political charge to dismantle diversity, equity, and inclusion efforts.

The harsh reality is that educators, who are responsible for the growth and development of children, are not united in their beliefs about anti-racist work. We know that educators exist who embrace and act on racist ideologies, which makes leading anti-racist efforts challenging for leaders of color. For instance, I have encountered educators who fully support ICE raids in schools and book bans when content relates to gender or race. As DEI practitioners of color, we often lead anti-racist work while experiencing racism within our institutions. We navigate colleagues' unchecked beliefs about race, while checking our own emotions to avoid being mislabled. We face conflicts when community members feel harmed by our mere presence. We experience racial trauma that can only be worked out through therapy. Therefore, we need to intentionally talk about systems of care and things we can do to restore our bodies and minds. Chapter 7 will focus on how we combat resistance and protect our peace. We must take care of ourselves while remaining true to our purpose.

Understanding the ADA and Combating Ableism in the Workplace

Section 504 of the Rehabilitation Act of 1973 was developed from the disability rights movement of the early 1970s (Bateman & Bateman, 2006). It was the first federal civil rights law to protect people with disabilities, laying the groundwork for the Americans with Disabilities Act (ADA). The ADA was a civil rights law passed in 1990 to prohibit discrimination against individuals with disabilities (Bateman & Bateman, 2006). This law ensured that people with disabilities had equal access to opportunities, including employment, transportation, public services, housing, telecommunications, and educational facilities. In 2008, the Americans with Disabilities Act (ADA) was amended to broaden the definition of 'disability,' extending protections and accommodations to a greater number of individuals whose conditions affect their capacity to perform or participate in activities (U.S. Equal Employment Opportunity Commission).

Many countries beyond the United States have enacted disability laws to eliminate discrimination and improve the quality of life for people with disabilities. The Equality Act of 2010 in the United Kingdom requires employers and service providers to provide accommodations to people with disabilities (Pyper & Uwazuruike, 2024). New Zealand's Disability Strategy maps out action steps to improve accessibility, health, education, employment, and engagement within communities for people with disabilities (Ministry of Social Development, 2016). The Accessibility for Ontarians with Disabilities Act (AODA) "offers guidelines for how to produce accessible texts, websites, and communications" (Parekh, 2022, p. 128). Furthermore, Canada passed the Accessible Canada Act in 2019 to promote accessibility and prevent discrimination.

The policies of disability justice call for DEI practitioners to identify and disrupt ableism in the workplace. Gillian Parekh (2022) defines ableism as "the privileging of ability that conditionally aligns human value to perceived ability, consequently devaluing disability and disabled people" (p. 12). It is the mistreatment or prejudice against individuals with disabilities, often resulting in exclusion from opportunities or services and marginalization.

Internalized ableism conditions people to believe that individuals with disabilities are incapable, inferior, or need saving (Villines, 2021). Those beliefs can lead to ableist language (often unintentional) or actions that disregard disabilities in policy or program development.

Ableist language is rhetoric used to reinforce stigmas and stereotypes about disabilities. It signals that being disabled is a deficiency. For instance, how often have you heard others (perhaps yourself) casually talk about their undiagnosed obsessive-compulsive disorder? *My OCD is showing again*! People may categorize their perceived negative habits as a condition, without ever acknowledging the lived experiences of individuals who do operate with OCD and receive treatments. As a result of the global pandemic, many of us conduct more meetings or business through virtual platforms (e.g., Zoom, Google Meets, Microsoft Teams, etc.) and commonly use the ableist word 'mute' in virtual spaces. We tell our colleagues to unmute their microphones without thinking about the implications of that language and its impact on people who identify as non-verbal. I learned that lesson the hard way while conducting a virtual workshop for professional development. After asking people to 'unmute' a few times, a participant lovingly called me in and encouraged me to say, "Can you turn on your microphone?" in place of the ableist language. We all have learning and unlearning to do as a part of our human condition. Figure 6.4 provides other examples of ableist language and ways to be inclusive. It is important to note that language is evolving. What may have been normalized in the past, can deeply insult or offend others in the present. Fortunately for us, we have the power and ability to refine our language in ways that center the humanity of all people. Figure 6.4 provides a list of language we can uproot and plant in our everyday conversations (Rahman, 2019).

Ableism can manifest at the institutional level through policies, systems, and the infrastructures of schools. There are school buildings that may lack universal designs to ensure that programs, technologies (e.g., websites, virtual platforms, etc.), and spaces are created to accommodate all students. For instance, videos on school websites may not have closed captioning or an accessible transcript for all people to retrieve information. School buildings may structurally lack ramps and spatial layouts that promote accessibility. From an instructional standpoint, ability grouping can yield to isolation if constructed in a way that leaves children feeling 'less than' and inadequate (ex. Teacher: *Only readers in the high group can read this book.*) Policies may also fail to recognize the accommodations students need to achieve learning, particularly if those policies are dismissive of mental health (ex. penalizing a student who was late to class for trying to manage their anxiety disorder).

Language to uproot	Language to plant in everyday conversations
Handicapped, crippled, deformed, the disabled, etc. Handicapped parking	Focus on people-first language that honors the humanity of the person. *He lives with a disability.* Accessible parking
Mute (ex. She's mute.)	Acknowledge the lived experiences of people who may be non-verbal or use devices to communicate. *She cannot verbalize her speech and uses a device to communicate her needs.* Virtual call: *Your microphone is turned off. Could you turn your microphone on?*
She/He/They is or are special ed.	Focus on the actual program rather than framing it as an adjective. *She receives special education services.* Note: The language 'functional needs' is preferred over special needs, yet many schools have traditional special education departments.
Referring to individuals as being retarded, a spaz, or crazy in common day language.	Refrain dehumanizing language. Acknowledge a person's condition. *She lives with a mental health condition/illness.*
Referring to individuals as 'normal.'	Do not signal that differences are a deficit or imply that people with disabilities are odd. Rather, use *non-disabled or people without a disability.*

Figure 6.4 Language to uproot and plant to combat ableism.

School celebrations, designed with good intentions, can also inadvertently perpetuate ableism. Halloween festivities can reflect individuals using one's culture or disability as a costume, making a mockery out of one's identity or condition. Many schools also host dances that involve bright lights, loud music, and crowded spaces that may not consider sensory needs for children or adults who are required to chaperone. Another common school-based event that vividly showcases ableism is the 100th Day of School celebration. Students are encouraged to dress as elderly individuals (promoting ageism) and use canes, walkers, and hearing aids as playful props. For families with children who rely on medical walking or hearing devices, such themed days can be discouraging. Rather than having students bring canes to school that are eventually used in sword fights and confiscated, we can have them engage in meaningful activities where they can sort, draw, or build 100 things. We could also just skip 100th Day celebrations altogether and honor the 67th Day of school (go ahead and say it, "six-seeeven"). No matter the approach, we must find ways to model the inclusive practices we promote.

Similar to Title IX and VI, combating ableism requires mirror work and education about disability rights. As DEI practitioners, we should be conscious of our own approaches, language, beliefs, and the infrastructures we build to ensure the promotion of accessibility and inclusion. Mirror work encourages us to think about the messages we have internalized about disabilities, including what we were taught or what we heard in our upbringings. It is important for us to consider our beliefs about disabilities and our ability to recognize ableism in overt and subtle forms. Circling back to my Zoom experience, I should have recognized the implications of my language. As DEI practitioners, we must deconstruct how ableism operates in us and our everyday lives. Here are some other practical things we can do in the workplace to combat ableism in addition to our own mirror work:

- **Disability awareness education and accessibility:** When selecting educational materials or designing professional development initiatives, it is essential to ensure that learning opportunities are accessible and responsive to the diverse needs of all individuals. Accessible learning materials include resources such as large-print handouts, captioned videos, and audio versions of presentations. We can also provide ongoing education that creates awareness of inclusive language, disabilities, accommodations, and universal design.
- **Advocate for policy changes:** Policies should not penalize or marginalize students or staff based on their conditions. Ensure that policies support the needs of people with disabilities, including rights to accommodations. When developing a policy ask, *How will this impact people with disabilities?*
- **Support universal design:** Create curricula and learning environments that are accessible to everyone. For students, this includes adaptable seating, digital content for accessibility, and varied methods for students to demonstrate learning.
- **Disrupt ableism in the moment:** When ableist practices emerge, we must feel confident in our approach to disrupt it. Leading by example encourages others to recognize and confront ableism as an institutional norm.
- **Leverage equity teams to combat ableism:** School-based and district equity teams should talk about ways to address ableism in educational systems. These teams can also elevate disability awareness through programs or learning experiences.

- **Community feedback and needs-assessments:** Recognizing institutional barriers that negatively impact individuals with disabilities is essential. By establishing spaces for input on accessibility and disability justice, we can better identify challenges and work towards effective solutions.

The work of deconstructing ableism in workspaces became personal after I was diagnosed with an autoimmune disorder. I did not realize how much systems were riddled with ableism until I developed a chronic illness after my first year of teaching. From staff activities that exacerbated health conditions to ableist language or stereotypes (ex. "You don't look like a sick person."), many leaders and colleagues throughout my educational career were not prepared to interact with people with disabilities or chronic health conditions, which ultimately made me question their ability to care for children with disabilities. I often found myself overexplaining why I could not participate in certain staff functions or activities, rather than having people create an experience with my immunocompromised identity in mind. When the COVID-19 pandemic emerged, I became overwhelmed from the realization that I was expendable. Parkeh's book, *Ableism in Education* (2022), discussed the apathy from societal messaging that assured people not to worry about the coronavirus unless they had an underlying condition. It implied that people without underlying health conditions could live their best lives, while the rest of us needed to hide under a rock. The platitude 'we're all in this together' was hurtful while feeling left behind and watching communities of people protest every protocol for safety. Living with a chronic illness has provided a unique lens to my leadership, yet it should not take a diagnosis (something impacting you personally or as a caregiver) to see how our educational systems and policies within society exclude or marginalize people with disabilities. Therefore, we all need to invest in mirror work and consider holistic approaches beyond policies to ensure that people with disabilities feel seen and have a sense of belonging.

Leading by Example

Organizational culture encompasses shared values, beliefs, and policies that inform behaviors. A school culture dedicated to anti-discrimination reflects educational leaders who set clear standards through their actions. When leaders quickly address incidents of discrimination or misconduct, it sends a strong message that malpractices or discriminatory acts are not tolerated and that people will be held accountable. Through focus groups, I have encountered educators who have expressed frustrations regarding their principal's lack of intervention in the face of harm. A number of these educators worked hard to create responsive classroom environments, often feeling unrecognized for their work. Meanwhile, some of their colleagues were known as integral members of the school community and praised despite their malpractices and overt prejudices that caused tension. As discussed in *Chapter 5*, when leaders refuse to hold people accountable, their inaction conveys that unacceptable behaviors are welcomed. What goes unchallenged, becomes endorsed.

An Interview with Imprint Legal Group Attorney, Jessica Heiser

As a DEI administrator at a district level who was responsible for the enforcement of Title IX and VI, I have worked with many attorneys for guidance while processing claims of discrimination. Jessica Heiser is an attorney who has become one of my good friends after working through many investigations and challenging situations together. We have co-facilitated dozens of presentations about various forms of discrimination, including sessions about the rights of students who identify as transgender. The thing I admire the most about Jessica is the equity lens she carries into her legal practices. She leads with integrity, which is why she left a law firm as a partner to start her own legal business that centers diversity, equity, and inclusion. I asked Jessica to share her expertise and answer a series of questions through an interview:

Q: How can DEI practitioners prevent ableism in the workplace?

Jessica: Ableism, like racism or sexism, is difficult to identify if you are non-disabled, but once you see it, you cannot unsee it. It is everywhere. It's the air we breathe. I like the suggestions about the language we use, but most ableism—like racism, sexism, xenophobia, you name it—is structural.

Because ableism is so ubiquitous, the easiest way to "lift the veil" and see it is to simply ask. The person with disabilities notices language, practices, and barriers on a daily basis that a non-disabled person will not. I worked for a legal organization that specialized in disability law and serving clients with disabilities, so we felt like we understood ableism pretty well. We gave ourselves a little pat on the back when we addressed issues like the use of restrictive practices on children with disabilities or when we called someone in about their language. But when we hired a law clerk who was blind, we realized that we were not fully "walking the walk." After the law clerk had worked for us for a few weeks and I had developed a good relationship with him, I asked him out to lunch and broached the topic with sensitivity: "James, I have noticed over the last few weeks that there were a few things we could have done better to be more accessible," I said. "Like when we started a meeting last week with new people, we should have had everyone introduce themselves and give a description of their physical appearance. I dropped the ball on that one. I'm also not sure if we're writing emails in the best way for a screen reader to read. Would you be willing to share anything else that we could have proactively done to make things more accessible for other people with limited vision?" (**Side note:** People with disabilities should not bear the burden of educating their workplace on how to be accessible—that burden is emotionally and physically heavy—so broach the topic respectfully and sensitively. And do not ask if you are not prepared to hear the answer and implement some of their suggestions.)

You'll notice that my question to the law clerk was about accessibility, not accommodations. Accommodations are asked for and legally provided (unless certain circumstances apply) to certain qualifying individuals with disabilities, but accessibility is proactively provided to all individuals through universal design. For example, an employer may provide a wheelchair ramp because a person with a wheelchair was hired and they needed to get around (that's an accommodation, legally required for one person). But an employer may also provide a wheelchair ramp because it helps all people with wheelchairs and mobility devices, babies in strollers, people pushing heavy carts or luggage (that's accessibility or universal design, not legally required, but helpful to many people).

Q: How can we support non-binary or transgender students or staff in this climate under current executive orders?

A: Let's start with the legalities: President Trump's administration fancies press releases with the fun title "executive order." Most of President Trump's executive orders are simply headline grabbers that are later found to be illegal and unenforceable. Executive orders cannot override federal laws or statutes (including the U.S. Constitution). The primary power of an executive order is *within* the federal government: When a president issues an executive order telling a federal agency, like the Department of Health and Human Services, what to do, that generally has a lot of legitimate power. But when the executive order tells private universities what to do, that is generally weak (and commonly illegal and struck down by the courts). Several executive orders recently issued about transgender and non-binary individuals are in conflict with federal law and will be struck down by the courts. I always urge school clients to exercise caution when reading any headlines about executive orders: DO NOT OVER COMPLY. Do not preemptively comply. Consult with your school attorney about what provisions are truly legally mandated. It is likely your attorney will say that you need to wait to make any changes until the lawsuits play out in court.

Apart from the legal analysis, I turn to the root of education: Safe children are learning children. Children who are physically and psychologically safe are able to focus on algebra; children who are in danger, hungry, or abused cannot. Regardless of what a presidential administration or federal judge tells us, every single staff member—from the principal to the custodial staff—has a moral, ethical, professional obligation to ensure every student is welcomed in their school building. Transgender and non-binary children are under enormous pressure right now, and it will only get worse before it gets better. When our trans children and immigrant children are the targets, we must ensure our school staff is ultra-sensitive to their inclusion. After 9/11, school leaders needed to ensure school environments were safe for our Muslim and Arab children. Whatever the current political target is, our school needs to be a safe place for those identifying children. Right now, we need to be making things as easy as possible for our trans kids: Stop differentiating between boys and girls in school, stop making bathrooms so odd and difficult to access, make sure all complaints of harassment or bullying are taken seriously, make sure every gender-nonconforming child has at least one staff member they are comfortable with, and evaluate mental health supports. These aren't revolutionary ideas, but they take time and effort. Our gender-nonconforming kids need that from us now.

A: What policy work is needed to ensure that environments are free of harassment or discrimination?

Jesscia: Policies are the floor, not the ceiling. They're the starting line. If a school lacks a solid policy, it is a red flag that they lack solid procedures and a solid culture.

Non-discrimination policies need to be reviewed on an annual basis, preferably by the school attorney working in collaboration with school administrators, who submits suggestions to the school board. School attorneys will typically write the policy to be as "bare bones" as possible, only addressing the legally mandated provisions. If a school administrator wants to add more, especially if it will help a class of students feel seen and heard, the administrator should tell the attorney why that language is important.

The policy needs to be incredibly easy to find on a school website and handbook. Front office staff in every building needs to know where to direct a parent who brings up a discrimination question.

But the policy is only the start. The policy needs to be supported by solid procedures, training and professional development, pulse surveys to students and staff, randomized audits or reviews of staff responses to concerning incidents, and case studies. These actions eventually lead to cultural shifts. I think of culture as "the way we do things around here and what we do when we think nobody is looking." That is really where you want to see change happen.

Q: How can DEI practitioners build capacity within schools to ensure that all employees and students cultivate environments free of discrimination or harassment?

Jessica: DEI practitioners have such huge lifts within schools. So first, I would tell all DEI practitioners to give yourselves grace and patience.

Second, build a coalition. Your goal is to make yourself obsolete: the change you want to see happen (an anti-racist, anti-ableist, anti-sexist school environment) needs to happen regardless of your presence, so building a coalition to effectuate cultural change is essential. Target unlikely candidates, not necessarily those in obvious power: perhaps the superintendent isn't "on board," but can you form alliances with the superintendent's administrative assistant (who, as we all know, carries significant soft power)? Do not neglect the food services staff, custodial staff, transportation staff, athletic coaches, and paraprofessionals. They are often overlooked in change management, and yet, they witness the most unstructured parts of a student's day—when harassment and discrimination are most likely to occur. (This certainly isn't a scientific measure, but anecdotally, for every discriminatory incident I have seen take place in a classroom, I have seen 100 discriminatory incidents take place in the locker room, on the bus, on the recess playground, or in the cafeteria. Most bullying and harassment happen in the unstructured environments and is witnessed by the bus driver ten times more than the classroom teacher.)

Third, engage students. Students are an untapped resource when it comes to making schools more inclusive. Ask students how they want to see their school be more inclusive, what ideas they have, what concerning incidents or language they've witnessed and how they reacted. Just as bus drivers are more likely to witness harassment than classroom teachers, students are even more likely to witness harassment than the bus driver. And they are also more likely than any adult in the building to understand what it feels like to feel left out.

Q: What advice would you give to DEI practitioners who are promoting inclusion under executive orders that call for the elimination of practices that promote educational justice?

Jessica: It is imperative that we consider the difference between legal requirements and cultural shifts or press releases. Do not over-comply or preemptively comply with executive orders or headlines. Do not allow your school to abandon its mission to educate and include all students out of fear or extreme caution.

We have never had laws in this country (U.S.) to promote inclusion in our schools. We have had laws since the 1960s that aim to <u>stop</u> bad actions in schools: stopping racial segregation, stopping discrimination on the basis of sex, stopping exclusion of students with disabilities. But our laws have not promoted inclusion or proactively integrated our schools. Inclusion has always been the work of people on the ground: our teachers, administrators, bus drivers, and custodians who prioritize relationships with all children. Our DEI practitioners take those relationships and build systems and structures. All of this has happened, and will continue to happen, in the backdrop of laws that—at best—aim to stop harm. The true work has always been ours.

Center Humanity in Our Practices

Although social emotional learning (SEL) has been a commonly held practice among students within schools, it is also a framework that needs to be embraced widely by adults. As DEI practitioners, we need to understand our emotions, the ways we manage stress and adversity, and how we connect with others. It is hard to foster a culture of empathy or respect within the workplace, if we are not aware of our own emotional intelligence. Figure 6.5 demonstrates the relationship between social emotional learning competencies (CASEL, 2020) and leadership in efforts to embrace humanizing approaches in equity work.

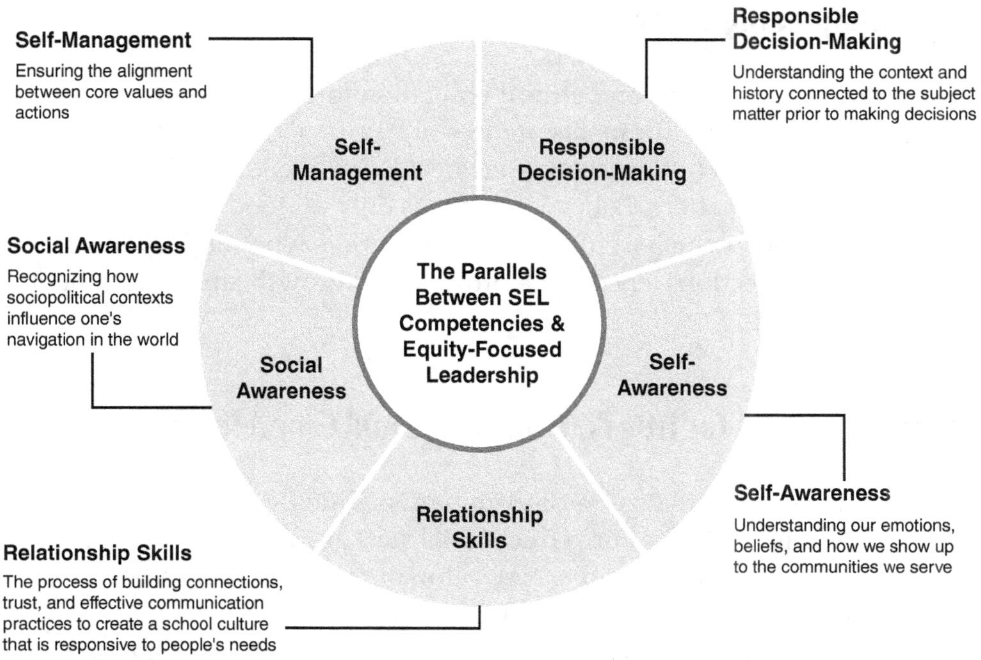

Figure 6.5 The Parallels between SEL and equity-focused leadership.

Equity-focused leadership requires a deliberate and thoughtful approach to engaging with communities. As DEI practitioners, we should feel compelled to respond to the emotional weight children or staff carry into school that disengages them from learning or productivity. We should feel compelled to remove barriers and allocate resources to help students thrive. We should feel compelled to extend care to the humans we serve.

Humanizing approaches require us to be conscious of the stories and lived experiences that people bring into environments. As DEI practitioners, we should feel empowered to acknowledge human experiences and to celebrate the cultural identities as well as histories of students and staff. When a catastrophic event affects a school community, it is important to acknowledge what is happening and communicate how our systems are helping those involved. We also know there are many cultural and religious observances that encompass the lives of our students and staff. It is important to honor cultural differences and to couple acknowledgement with accountability. For instance, acknowledging Yom Kippur in educational contexts means creating schedules that do not exclude Jewish students or staff from school-based events. We can support school leaders to center the humanity of people in their decision-making. Importantly, we can continue to show up for the communities we serve, despite the constant assaults on human rights within our political climate.

Chapter Highlights

1. We all hold a moral and ethical obligation to ensure that working and learning environments are free of harassment and forms of discrimination (e.g., racism, sexism, ableism, etc.).
2. Leadership matters. Policy language is only as good as its enforcers. Building an inclusive culture requires leaders who model justice, foster connections, encourage professional growth, and hold others accountable.

Additional Pro-tips for Title IX, Title VI, and ADA Coordinators

1. Know your district's non-discrimination, Title IX, Title VI, and ADA policies. Make sure educational staff are also knowledgeable of policies and procedures. Not following procedures can harm students and staff, and result in lawsuits.
2. Find learning opportunities that will keep you abreast of current federal, state, or local policies. For instance, I have attended

quite a few Title IX workshops through the Association of Title IX Administrators which offers comprehensive case studies and resources to support investigative work. Some school districts may cover travel and/or registrations for professional learning experiences.

3. Make sure to contact a local child protective agency when claims of sexual harassment, assault, and forms of abuse surface in reports that involve minors.
4. Document everything within an investigation. Note the dates and times of interviews, phone calls, meeting cancellations-EVERYTHING! Our roles are complex and we are constantly moving from one thing to the next. Therefore, we cannot rely on our memory to recall critical details.
5. Work closely with families from both parties following a formal complaint. Be transparent about procedures, systems of support, and offer internal as well as external resources (e.g., mental health support, etc.).
6. Do not hesitate to reach out to attorneys who work within your school district. I never hesitated to call attorneys when needed as a layer of protection for myself!

Mirror Work

1. Take the time to revisit Figure 6.3. What did you learn about yourself? What support do you need to lead racial justice efforts in schools?
2. Disability justice mirror work:
   - What are your beliefs about disabilities?
   - What language do you use while describing people with disabilities or their experiences?
   - How do you support the rights of people with disabilities and eliminate ableism in the workplace?

References

Apfelbaum, E. P., Pauker, K., Sommers, S. R., & Ambady, N. (2010). In blind pursuit of racial equality? *Psychological Science*, *21*(11), 1587–1592https://doi.org/10.1177/0956797610384741.

Bender, M. (2016, October 3). Yale study tests implicit bias of preschool teachers. Yale News. https://yaledailynews.com/articles/yale-study-tests-implicit-bias-of-preschool-teachers

Bateman, B., & Bateman, C. F. (2006). *A principal's guide to special education*. 2nd ed. Council for Exceptional Children.

Boschert, S. (2022). *37 words: Title IX and fifty years of fighting sex discrimination*. The New Press.

Buchanan-Rivera, E. (2022). *Identity affirming classroom: Spaces that center humanity*. Routledge Publishing.

CASEL. (2020). *Casel's SEL framework*. https://casel.org/casel-sel-framework-11-2020/

Combahee River Collective. (1977). The Combahee River Collective Statement. https://americanstudies.yale.edu/sites/default/files/files/Keyword%20Coalition_Readings.pdf

Equal Opportunity Employment Commission. ADA Amendment Act of 2008. https://www.eeoc.gov/statutes/ada-amendments-act-2008

Heiser, J., Interview. 28 August 2025.

Henry-Dixon, N. (2021, August 30). Racial segregation of Black people in Canada. *The Canadian Encyclopedia*. https://thecanadianencyclopedia.ca/en/article/racial-segregation-of-black-students-in-canadian-schools

Ighodaro, E., & Wiggan, G. (2013). *Curriculum violence: America's new civil rights issue* (Education in a Competitive and Globalizing World). Nova Novinka.

Interactive Institute for Social Change. (2025). Racial Affinity Group Field Guide. https://interactioninstitute.org/wp-content/uploads/2025/10/IISC-Affinity-Group-Field-Guide_Oct2025.pdf

Jones, S. (2020). *Ending curriculum violence*. SPLC. https://www.splcenter.org/resources/stories/ending-curriculum-violence/

Ministry of Social Development. (2016). New Zealand disability strategy. https://www.abuseincare.org.nz/assets/Evidence-library/Part-1/Office-for-Disability-Issues-New-Zealand-Disability-Strategy-2016-2026-November-2016.pdf

Parekh, G. (2022). *Ableism in education: Rethinking school practices and policies*. Routledge Publishing.

Pyper, D., & Uwazuruike, A. (2024, December 2). *A short introduction to equality law and policy*. House of Commons Library. https://researchbriefings.files.parliament.uk/documents/CBP-9448/CBP-9448.pdf

Rahman, L. (2019). *Disability language guide*. Standford Disability Initiative Board. https://ccla-web.s3.amazonaws.com/files/resources/disability-inclusive-language-guide.pdf

Richards, M. (2020, February 10). How a lack of inclusive sex education and a reliance on pornography leave LGBTQ youth facing greater risks than their straight peers. The 74. https://www.the74million.org/article/how-a-lack-of-inclusive-sex-education-and-a-reliance-on-pornography-leave-lgbtq-youth-facing-greater-risks-than-their-straight-peers/

Stevenson, B. (2018). *Just mercy: A true story of the fight for injustice.* [Adaptation for Young Adults] Penguin Random House.

Urban, W. J., & Wagoner, J. L. (2014). *American education: A history* (5th ed.). Routledge.

Villines, Z. (2021, November 8). What is ableism, and what is its impact?" Medically reviewed by Debra Sullivan, Ph.D. Medical News Today. https://www.medicalnewstoday.com/articles/ableism

7

Navigating Adversity

How We Resist and Protect Our Peace

In Chapter 5, we learned that systems are human created with interlocking components, including norms, policies, practices, and power dynamics, that shape the status quo. The existing conditions within systems, whether flawed or effective, provide a sense of predictability and deeply influence human behaviors. People have a tendency to align themselves with the status quo, settling into established routines and cultural norms. When people rely on familiarity and become accustomed to operating in a particular way, change will inevitably yield to pushback and various forms of resistance.

As DEI practitioners, we must recognize that resistance is an intrinsic response to change when people feel instability, discomfort, or fear of loss. Resistance also becomes stronger when people do not understand the rationale behind change, or believe new initiatives undermine their work or go against their beliefs. We will encounter people within the workplace who will respond to our efforts with criticism, skepticism, and passionate anger. Some educators may refuse to acknowledge institutional racism, their role in perpetuating inequities, and the importance of self-awareness.

Resistance typically indicates either a gap in understanding or unmet needs, prompting us to actively listen to others and offer clarification as needed. Moments of resistance also compel us to shine a light on the status quo and how it does not benefit all members of a school community, opening the door for critical conversations and educational opportunities. Personally, I used to struggle with pushback. I wanted people to understand my

DOI: 10.4324/9781032623542-7

intentions, find value in my efforts, and frankly, like me as a person. The criticisms and hostile actions from people in opposition of my work were soul-crushing. However, my mentors would remind me that resistance was an indication of progress. It is our signal that change is happening and that people are paying attention. I eventually learned that resistance does not necessarily indicate personal failure but rather invites us to be strategic in our approaches and interactions with others.

Black scholar, activist, and writer, bell hooks (2001), reminds us that the heart of justice is truth telling. We must confront opposition with truth, and reclaim our power through connections, storytelling, and radical self-love. Navigating adversity in an anti-DEI climate requires proactive and strategic work, resilience, and community mobilization. Although we cannot predict every challenge we will face, we can mentally prepare for controversy and learn how to overcome adversity with our integrity and wellness intact.

Knowing When to Push, Pause, and Protect Our Peace

When I started my first position as a Chief Equity and Inclusion Officer, there were only two principals of color within the district, one who identified as a Black woman. Crystal Thorpe was the first Black principal in the district and Hamilton County. She is an award-winning educational leader who has served in multiple leadership organizations, including her former role as president of the Indiana Association of School Principals. Thorpe authored the article, *Leading While Black (2022)* for the National Association of Secondary School Principals which discussed her journey as a Black woman in leadership. The following is an excerpt from the article that also provides a glimpse of my onboarding experience:

> *As a principal, I have been publicly humiliated, silenced, minimized, and ignored. I have served under more than six superintendents during my tenure. A superintendent once tossed peanut butter crackers at me during an administrative team meeting because my school raised the least amount of money for a fundraiser. Another principal received a cake for his "excellent job" of fundraising. A week later, the superintendent apologized, but the peanut butter crackers are still in my desk drawer.*

Her personal account of public humiliation is an experience I will never forget, because it was my first administrative team meeting within the district, and I witnessed the exchange firsthand. There was anxious laughter throughout the room and a locking of eyes among colleagues that indicated discomfort. However, the discomfort of colleagues did not compare to Thorpe's emotions that I deeply understood as a Black woman in that moment. I was not familiar with many colleagues or schools yet knew that Thorpe led a junior high that had the most students of color and families with financial insecurities. The distribution of crackers and the lack of consideration for Crystal's positionality as a Black woman within a predominantly white environment highlighted the tension between DEI and organizational culture. Existing norms, power structures, and mindsets do not change because of the appointment of a DEI administrator or the promotion of equity work. Rather, inequitable systems and practices change through equity-principled leadership and the collective will of people to move in solidarity.

I also thought about my positionality as a new Black administrator, who had not even been introduced to staff and watched harm unfold. What could I have done in that moment? I did not fully understand the context or relationship dynamics that existed in the room, yet should I have said something? *Hi everyone, you don't know me yet and I'm sure I'll be introduced later in the agenda, but I just wanted to point out the microaggression that just took place and have a teachable moment.* What if I read Thorpe's reaction wrong and she wasn't offended by the peanut butter crackers? What if the exchange was an inside joke that I did not understand as a new employee? My internal struggle during that meeting and onboarding experience illustrates the political and institutional landscapes that DEI practitioners navigate daily. We are immersed in contexts where we must thoughtfully assess situations, interactions, and dispositions to determine strategic problem-solving approaches. When knowledge gaps and mirror work are lacking among people in positions of leadership, we must also consider how we confront power.

A common challenge that many DEI practitioners face is *knowing when to push, knowing when to pause, and knowing when it's time to protect our peace* (Buchanan-Rivera, 2022). There are moments when we cannot remain silent or complicit. Sometimes we must embrace vulnerability and courage to stop one's abuse of power or actions that cause marginalization. We stand up for what is just and humane, knowing the risks that come with attempts to disrupt the status quo. There are other times when we need to pause and collect our thoughts or accountability partners to debrief action steps. We cannot leap into action with every alert and must condition our bodies to be mindful in efforts to protect our stamina and the energy we bring into this work. Circling back to the administrative meeting, that was a time where I chose to pause, ask questions (especially about the relationship dynamics), and build connections, particularly with Thorpe, who is now a dear friend. We do not need to react to everything and should give ourselves the space and time to complete meaningful assessments.

There are also times when we must protect our peace, recognizing when oppressive conditions are impacting our wellness and mental health. We may need to define our boundaries, letting go of connections or circumstances that deplete our energy. Protecting our peace means that we unapologetically choose ourselves, prioritizing calm over chaos. We choose to combat push-back through our own acts of resistance, including rest and seeking joy.

The administrative meeting and incident of public humiliation foreshadowed the backlash, media publications, threats, and petitions that would soon emerge against my work without the support of leadership, especially school board members. Without buy-in from leadership in any position, it can be difficult to enact meaningful change within educational systems. When our efforts are not supported or continuously sabotaged to a point where our bodies feel the weight of political unrest, we may need to think about what peace looks like in action.

Many of us grapple with our navigation within systems of inequity. We may struggle with the timing of our advocacy or our approach (push). Some of us may also have difficulties reading the room (pause) or our bodies (peace) while engaging in work-related activities. There have been times where I have pushed so hard for equitable outcomes at work that I had nothing left to give once home with my family—*living in a constant state of weariness*. We need to talk about our emotional well-being and the costs that come with the fight for justice in this climate. We also need to acknowledge the toll it takes on our bodies to constantly play offense and defense under leadership or governance that works to eradicate or hinder our efforts. Leading in oppressive conditions takes courage. Speaking truth in an era where misinformation is widely embraced takes courage.

Preparing for Adversity: Get Your Mind Right

While scrolling through social media platforms, I often see memes that describe the initial perceptions of jobs, parenting, or relationships versus the reality (ex. *what I thought this would look like vs. what it looks like in reality*). For instance, some of us may have thought that parenting would reflect children who actively listen and adhere to our guidance. We may not have anticipated the creative, free-spirited child, who takes it upon herself to dig a toy screwdriver into your wall out of pure curiosity—which may or may not have happened in my home. Similarly, many of us take on DEI roles with a spirit of optimism. We freedom dream (Kelley, 2002) and think about what schools could be with equitable resources, policies, and practices. Although we know that challenges are inevitable with any new experience, we may not anticipate the depths of adversity we will encounter and the lengths some people or groups will go to hinder DEI efforts or to protect whiteness.

Mental preparation for leading DEI work involves us visualizing accomplished goals and possibilities as well as potential roadblocks. For instance, we need to anticipate working with individuals in internal and external systems who believe DEI means giving handouts to people of color at the cost of harming white people. We need to expect potential disruptions within professional learning experiences when participants disagree with the content being presented. We need to consider how to protect ourselves when people's fear compels them to abandon us while we're at the frontlines advocating for change. If we can identify potential barriers, we can focus our mental energy on the things we can control or influence to engage in proactive work.

One of the most important things we can do to combat resistance is to stay grounded in our beliefs about justice. Our beliefs serve as an internal compass that bring clarity and focus to our strategies and actions. When we are tempted to remain silent to avoid conflicts, our convictions and commitment to justice compel us to speak truth to power. There have been moments in my professionalism where I worried about consequences for speaking my truth. Then, I remembered my beliefs about the rights of children and elevated my voice. Resistance can make us second-guess our efforts and decision-making. For example, we may question if some issues are worth the battle when navigating relentless forces of opposition. If we are cognizant of our beliefs about justice and consider the humanity of all people, we can drown out the noises of opposition with the clarity of our mission. Resilience is activated when we adhere to core values (ex. inclusion over bigotry) that remind us of our why and what matters.

In a previous chapter, I talked about my experience at a school board meeting where board members debated whether to acknowledge gender in a non-discrimination policy. This meeting became a national headline. Many students attended the board meeting and advocated for policy changes. Trans students openly shared their stories, conveying why policies should acknowledge their lived experiences. In response to their advocacy, board members publicly debated their humanity. As students were told their lives were a phase or a product of confusion, I took it upon myself to escort students out of the boardroom to shield them from the transphobic language of adults. I hugged students as they sobbed on my shoulders and questioned why adults in positions of power in an educational setting would intentionally hurt them.

The day after the school board meeting, my superintendent talked to me about my interactions with students during the session. It was a scolding. I

Mental Preparation for DEI Practitioners
1. How can I focus on courageous actions instead of fear? 2. What strengths or skills do I possess to navigate controversy productively? 3. What does conflict resolution look like in my everyday life? 4. When controversial situations or conflicts emerge, do I understand the historical, social, and political contexts related to the problem? 5. What practices help me to stay grounded in the face of resistance? 6. How do I operate under pressure and resistance?

Figure 7.1 Mental preparation for DEI practitioners.

was told that my response to protect and nurture children was inappropriate. Apparently, I was too emotionally invested and needed to work on my leadership. This could have been a moment where I remained silent to avoid conflict (or potential reprimands, as we often worry about), but I decided to speak up for myself and shared how demonstrating empathy and humility is leadership. As a part of my core values and lived experiences, I lead to ensure that each child feels seen, heard, and valued. I am also reminded by Audre Lorde (1984) that when we dare to be powerful and walk in our mission, it becomes less important if we are afraid.

Figure 7.1 can help us think about the mental preparation that is needed for resiliency while navigating adversity. It is important to consider our core values, what is in our control, and how we analyze situations as they arise. Sometimes, we can filter situations through a limited lens that does not allow us to understand the full context prior to making decisions. Therefore, it is important for us to be perceptive and active listeners to ensure our belief systems center justice and not our own biases or egos. We are human and can get things wrong too.

Developing an Ancestor Playbook

Ancestral leadership is a philosophy that empowers us to uphold the values of ancestors who stewarded a vision for liberatory work. We consider how equity-principled leadership actions of the past influence our efforts to advance educational justice in the present. From our ancestors' labor and determination, we can carry the belief that each of us holds power to change systems. Grassroots movements, abolitionists, and collectivist approaches have demonstrated that it is possible to dismantle legally codified forms of injustice. Stories of teacher activism encourage us to carry our light and truth into pedagogical practices and spaces where decisions are made. As DEI practitioners, we can learn about activism from historical contexts and the wisdom of elders who empowered others to engage in collective responsibility.

For over 400 years, as noted in colonization, chattel slavery, Jim Crow laws, and redlining, racism and dehumanization have been prevalent within economic, legal, and educational systems. Our history reflects powerful stories of activism and resistance, including rebellions, protests, boycotts, covert organizing, and marches in response to injustice. The principles that embody liberatory work—*equity, inclusion, justice, access, and belonging*—were deeply rooted in ancestral leadership with the purpose of nurturing and sustaining communities. Although we may face hostility, isolation, or have moments of self-doubt, the stories of ancestors remind us that change is possible. Ancestral advocacy and resistance inspire us to lead with courage and love for humanity. We can put down the feeling of helplessness and build coalitions. We can put down the belief that educational justice is unachievable and apply pressure. The advancement of diversity, equity, and inclusion are not abstract principles, but rather living practices that have historical legitimacy marked by the fight of our ancestors.

Mental preparation for adversity also requires us to tap into the wisdom of ancestors. Sometimes we need to pause and intentionally reflect on our leadership. There are many lessons we can learn from ancestors who advocated for human and civil rights in the face of colonialism, racism, fascism, and oppressive conditions. The leadership of ancestors who led movements for justice was often rooted in community, freedom, and love for humanity. Ancestral leadership reminds us of our inner strength and calls for us to think about the legacy we want to build for an inclusive society. Many of our ancestors risked their lives to protect their land, culture, livelihood, language, and communities. Ancestral leadership inspires us to challenge power dynamics that perpetuate harm and reminds us that we can do hard things.

Ancestors of educational movements believed that education was the key to liberation and empowerment. They recognized that schools were political institutions and used teaching as an act of resistance. Ancestral educators of liberatory work honored storytelling, language, and culture in educational contexts, not the erasure of one's identity or lived experiences. We can learn from their stories and gain insightful lessons about stewarding a vision, endurance, and the courage needed for activism.

Some of us may have ancestors in mind who guide our steps and root us in our purpose. Civil rights activist Ella Baker has been a guiding light for my work when organizing community coalitions. She was pivotal in the development of the Student Nonviolent-Coordinating Committee (SNCC) and empowered young leaders with tools and skills to build a movement for justice. We all need an ancestral playbook as a part of our mental preparation as DEI practitioners. There is power in wisdom that can direct and refine our leadership. Consider the following questions in Figure 7.2 to help shape your ancestral leadership playbook:

Reflective Questions for Our Ancestral Playbook
Consider ancestors who were activists of liberatory work to advance equitable practices, equality, and inclusion. 1. Which ancestors do I hold in high esteem for their exemplary leadership? 2. How did ancestors navigate adversity? 3. What strategies did ancestors use amid controversy, threats, or resistance? 4. What aspects of their leadership do I want to emulate in my practices? 5. Which lessons do I want to carry from the wisdom of ancestors when faced with challenges? 6. How did ancestors care for themselves or their communities under oppressive conditions? 7. How will I build on the legacies of ancestors? 8. What legacy do I want to leave behind? What do I want to be remembered for? 9. What kinds of risks am I prepared to accept when engaging in activism or advocacy? 10. Would my ancestors be proud of my leadership actions and decision-making?

Figure 7.2 Reflective questions for our ancestral playbook.

Figure 7.3 demonstrates examples of individuals who paved the way for liberatory work in education. When the weight of today's sociopolitical environment leaves us feeling helpless, remembering the struggles our ancestors faced can inspire us to find strength and continue their legacy. At times, we must embrace courage, put on a shield of truth, and move forward despite challenges. Our ancestors demonstrated how to pursue progress even when confronted with hardship. It's vital to reclaim our strength, recognizing that barriers do not have to hold us back.

Ancestral leadership demonstrates that progress and systemic change require acts of resistance, courage, community organizing, and innovation. Standing up for human rights, particularly in educational systems, is not a newfound approach. Historically, the principles of DEI and variations of the acronym have remained a constant thread in the stories of freedom struggles. As practitioners of liberatory work, we need to embrace history to have a sense of identity within our roles. We need to honor those who came before us. Knowing our history and collective responses to injustice matter as we strive to work in partnership and hold each other accountable.

As noted in the ancestral stories (Figure 7.3), the pursuit of just educational systems will come with risks. Some of the risks in the historical accounts included violence, imprisonment, or even death. As a part of our mental

Educational Changemakers		
Mela Leger (1928–2006)	Manuelita de Atocha Romero (Mela) was born in Villanueva, New Mexico (New Mexico Historic Women Marker Program, 2026). As a monolingual Spanish speaker, education was not responsive to her needs despite anti-discrimination language in New Mexico's constitution. She earned a sociology degree from Loretto Heights College and a teaching certificate from New Mexico Highlands University. Dedicated to bilingual education, she mobilized the community to create a program for Spanish-speaking children and successfully advocated for guidelines in the Bilingual Education Act of 1973.	**Mela Leger reminds us that we can build coalitions to change policies and outcomes for children.**
Loris Malaguzzi (1920–1994)	Loris Malaguzzi was born in Correggio in 1920 under an Italian fascist dictatorship. Malaguzzi believed that democracy was brought to life through pedagogy and relationships (Malaguzzi, 1998; Gandini et. al., 2015). His leadership was the driving force behind the Infant-toddler Centres and Preschools of Reggio Emilia. The Reggio Emilia philosophy focuses on the power of children and their capabilities via child-centered approaches rooted in democracy. Malaguzzi expressed that early childhood environments should be spaces where freedom is practiced.	**Malaguzzi reminds us that schools can be places where freedom and democracy are practiced.**
Septima Clark (1898–1987)	Septima Poinsette Clark was born in Charleston, SC (Charron, 2012). Although she was a qualified teacher, Black people were not hired to teach in Charleston public schools. In 1916, she became a teacher in Johns Island, SC. After returning to Charleston in 1919, Clark partnered with the NAACP to advocate for the hiring of Black teachers which changed local laws. Clark taught until she was fired from her teaching job in 1956 for her involvement in the NAACP. She established Citizenship Schools that helped Black people with literacy, math, voter registration, and other citizenship rights (Theoarris, 2018).	**Clark prompts us to walk in our values and truth.** We can empower communities in impactful ways.

Figure 7.3 Educational changemakers. *(Continued)*

Educational Changemakers		
Harry (1905–1951) and Harriette Moore (1902-1952)	Harry and Harriette Moore were educators in Florida who were actively fighting for civil rights. In the 1940s, Moores founded a branch of the NAACP in Brevard County (Wilkerson, 2020; Allen, 2022). The Moores advocated for equal pay among Black teachers despite segregation. Harry Moore also fought for voting rights, investigated lynchings, and spoke out against police brutality. The Moores eventually were fired from their teaching positions due to their activism. During Harry Moore's tenure within the NAACP, Florida had the highest number of Black registered voters. On Christmas and the night of their wedding anniversary, the Moores were both killed by a bomb that was placed underneath their home (Harry was killed instantly, while Harriette died days later from injuries).	**The Moores teach us that activism should not only live within the schoolhouse, but within our everyday lives.** We are also reminded of the risks that come with activism, including loss of opportunities, threats, and violence.
Marva Collins (1936–2015)	Marva Collins was known for her transformative work in Chicago when she founded the Westside Preparatory School in 1975 (Collins & Tamarkin, 1990). She was motivated to start her own school after witnessing how public education systems were failing Black children. She held the unwavering belief that there was potential in every child and believed in their capabilities. Her innovations, curriculum, and approaches to teaching significantly improved student performance and gained national attention.	**Marva Collins reminds us to engage in innovative actions that honor the gifts and potential of all children.** We should feel empowered to change systems when needs are not being met.

Figure 7.3 (*Continued*)

preparation (Figure 7.2), we do need to ask ourselves the question about the *risks we are willing to take* as a part of our activism. It is important for me to emphasize that I am not advocating for anyone to fight at the cost of losing their family, health insurance, or livelihood. We need to be realistic with ourselves and ask how far we are willing to go for just conditions in schools. We need to mentally prepare for risks and consider the losses we are willing to accept. With a working spouse in my household, losing a job to uphold my integrity is a risk I am willing to take. Ending friendships or connections with people who refuse to see the humanity of others or uphold racist ideologies is another risk I am willing to take. As a consultant, I do believe that *all money isn't good money*, and I will decline opportunities with organizations that are misaligned with my values. We need time for self-talk and mirror work to understand what we stand for and what we stand against, considering the risks we are willing to embrace. The following statements explore how fellow DEI practitioners navigate resistance:

> ***Meet it head on. Do not apologize for doing the work.*** *Leverage the community that is fed up with schools and systems for not doing the work. For example, when my district opened the DuBois Academy (open to all male students with a focus on Afrocentric curriculum) many white people were saying that the school was racist and supported segregation. Some went as far as to say that Martin Luther King Jr. would oppose a school that targets the needs of Black boys. The Black community, that has history of being marginalized, silenced, and mistreated by the public schools in America, rallied and supported the school. Threats were made on my life. Some Black people got scared and backed away from being a part of the school. The school is thriving and the young men that attend the 6-12 school are doing well academically. -John Marshall, Chief Equity Officer, Kentucky*

> ***I think it is essential to be clear on your mission and values.*** *We have refined ours as a school, and I feel we all stand strong on those convictions. We do not hide who we are or what work we do as a school. Families, teachers, board members, and any other stakeholders understand from the get-go who we are and what we stand for. We are also clear on what we expect from each stakeholder when it comes to incorporating our DEI work. A more concrete example is that at each staff meeting and board meeting we talk about our community agreements. We remind ourselves of our expectations for engagement. At our board and admin meetings, we review our strategic plans and examine how we are honoring our commitment to DEI work through these goals. We hold each other responsible for the work, and support each other in the implementation. -Penny Robbins, Executive Director of Preschool of the Arts, Wisconsin*

Dealing with Pushback, Resistance, and Anti-DEI Policies

Resistance has been a common challenge in DEI work that has been amplified in recent years with the weaponization of equity literacy. In our political climate, the mentioning of the words 'equity' or 'DEI' evokes emotional responses and misinformation. We have witnessed DEI misinterpretations that span from Black people being referred to as DEI hires (being less qualified and receiving positions solely based on race) to fonts on Microsoft Word (apparently, Calibri is too woke). There are people who have firm and uninformed beliefs about the purpose of DEI work, refusing to open their hearts or even pages within a book to gain a different perspective. Dealing with resistance requires emotional intelligence, work to combat propaganda, and strategic approaches to build community.

As a reminder, while engaging in liberatory work, there are times when we must push, pause, or protect our peace. Instead of reacting to every situation or statement shared, sometimes we need to pause to generate a space between stimuli and our response. Throughout the years, I have worked heavily on my emotional regulation while working with contentious adults. I used to allow people's words to affect me and would often go home, tearfully replaying situations to process what I could have done differently. Now, I have conditioned myself to seek clarity prior to outwardly showing an emotional response. I am strategic in my approach and use questions to redirect someone's venom or uninformed generalizations into a teachable moment of mirror work. Here's an example of handing someone a mirror:

Person A: I'm glad the president is getting rid of the illegals and this DEI work.
Person B: (Annoyed on the inside, calm on the outside) I do not consider any human being as an 'illegal,' it's not the language I use to describe a person. What is your issue with diversity, equity, or inclusion? Do you have a problem with diversity? Is it equity or inclusion?
Person A: They are taking all the jobs and I am glad they are going back.
Person B: Who is taking all the jobs? Could you tell me the community you are referencing?
Person A: The Mexicans.
Person B: Interesting. Do you have the statistics or data to verify that Mexicans are taking all of the jobs? Could you clarify which jobs?
Person A: I don't know the numbers off the top of my head, but it's happening every day.
Person B: Do you know of someone personally who lost their job because of this supposed influx of Mexicans who are seeking jobs?
Person A: Well, I don't, but I know it's happening.
Person B: It sounds like you know a lot of things that are happening without any personal accounts or credible information. Let me know when you have factual information to share.

When I hand people a mirror, it relieves me from reacting defensively and elevating my blood pressure. The interactive conversations from my experiences also confirm that many people base opinions on pure ignorance, rather than factual information. Resistance often emerges from one's lack of knowledge. It is easier for a person to embrace propaganda rather than to do their own homework and research. When I join a critical conversation, I clarify questionable rhetoric and ask questions. I uphold my boundaries and professionalism, even if a speaker's message feels like a personal attack. There are people who may want table-flipping, reality television controversy in their lives, but I refuse to be emotionally dysregulated and give anyone the satisfaction of drawing an unsavory reaction from me. When dealing with pushback, we must check ourselves and stay true to our values.

Truth Telling Campaigns

A systematic strategy may be necessary to facilitate understanding among members of a school community regarding the objectives, execution, and rationale of DEI initiatives. As misinformation and lack of knowledge often contribute to opposition, targeted education and enhanced awareness can address misconceptions about DEI and foster more informed perspectives. Truth-telling campaigns promote transparency, education, and ensure accountability. School districts must tell their story, illustrating how DEI is defined in schools and how it aligns with the mission.

The following outlines steps DEI practitioners can take to initiate truth-telling campaigns based on specific scenarios. I have purposefully provided a wide range of contexts, knowing that the pendulum will eventually shift on the side of justice. There will be a time when people are no longer fearful of repercussions for saying diversity, equity, or inclusion. We can prepare for today and tomorrow at the same time.

Dealing with Misconceptions about DEI

> **Scenario:** *Community stakeholders bombard central office and school administrators with calls or e-mails about their concerns with DEI (or CRT, gender ideology, etc.).*

Here are the steps DEI practitioners can take to combat misinformation:

1. **Identify the existing misconceptions that exist about DEI work within your school district.** Here are some examples that have crossed my desk whether from staff or families:
   - "DEI only benefits people of color."
   - "DEI means that we lower standards to diversify organizations."

- "DEI work exists to make children loathe their country and its history."
- "DEI makes white people look like villains in discussions about race and in turn, makes white children feel uncomfortable."
- "DEI only centers race."

2 **Devise a rebuttal to misconceptions, highlighting efforts that are actually happening within schools based on district goals.** Work with district equity teams and established school-community coalitions to develop talking points with actual data, personal stories, and testimonies that dispute misconceptions and offer different perspectives.

3 **Determine how you will convey and distribute information or testimonies related to DEI.** Here are some strategies aimed at advancing DEI initiatives and addressing misunderstandings:
   - Superintendents in collaboration with DEI administrators could schedule a 'state of the district address' where data and district updates are shared. This session could also include a response to parental concerns.
   - A school district could invest in a promotional video that showcases the perspectives of students to examine why DEI work is relevant and matters.
   - An internal document with talking points could be created for principals as a tool to address phone calls or e-mail concerns with similar themes. This may involve preparing a standardized response for principals or providing a template message that allows leaders to incorporate initiatives specific to their building in order to address and correct misinformation. (ex. Canned responses: *We are not licensed medical professionals and do not have the ability to perform gender surgeries in our school facilities … We select textbooks and supplemental materials that align with state standards. You can access a copy of the state standards from the following link if you have concerns regarding the lessons that were implemented.*)

4 **Continue to highlight or make DEI work visible as an ongoing endeavor.** Work with a school district's public relations team to think about the narration of DEI work throughout the district. Market events, student or parent testimonies, school partnerships, learning experiences, or staff awards that promote the district's mission as related to DEI work. Ongoing press releases of positive experiences and progress toward goals, creates a culture of transparency that is needed to combat the misrepresentation of DEI work.

Misalignment Between Vision and Actions

> **Scenario:** *You discover that your beliefs about justice and equity are misaligned from members of your leadership team. Although the district's mission conveys the importance of meeting the needs of all students and providing equal access to resources, colleagues continuously reveal their deficit ideologies about students (and their caregivers) through their language and decision-making.*

Critical conversations are inevitable while working with humans who carry different belief systems from their lived experiences. It is incredibly challenging to call in colleagues or people in positions of power because of potential changes in relationship dynamics following a dialogue. In situations where harm is revealed through language or actions, we are faced with choices. We can be silent and complicit, or we can raise our voices to strengthen educational systems and safeguard communities against marginalization. Either choice has its risks. The following ideas (a culmination of concepts learned from Chapters 4 and 5) share how DEI practitioners can foster a culture where critical conversations live.

Proactive Work (Cultivating Culture for Critical Conversations):

1 **Develop time for leadership development that centers critical conversations.** Propose a structure that allocates time for collaboration among school and/or district leaders. This would be a time where educational leaders could build trust, engage in scenario-based work, and practice critical conversations as a collective. The critical conversation series could center the mental preparation, language, strategies, and dispositions needed for mindful communication. School leaders can also share real-time situations with the intent of receiving guidance. Ongoing learning experiences that invite participants to practice courageousness, conditions leaders to effectively navigate conflict instead of avoiding it.

2 **Develop protocols for mindful communication.** Prior to scenario-based practices, encourage educational leaders to discuss what they need to have vulnerable conversations. Develop protocols for group dynamics. In team discussions, it may be helpful to agree upon the use of a buzzword or catchphrase to signal that a statement needs unpacking or a counterpoint. For example, I have been a part of leadership sessions where members have called for an "intentional pause" to further process comments or to ask questions. (Ex. *Hey! I need an intentional pause for clarity. What did you mean when you said? … I'm trying to understand.*)

3 **Invite school leaders to hold each other accountable.** When school leaders participate in scenario-based practices, provide time for collaboration and debriefing. Leaders should give each other constructive feedback on their approaches and language used in critical conversations. (Ex. Feedback: *You never addressed the issue or concern in a direct way. You danced around the issue.)*

Speaking Truth in the Moment (Misalignment between vision and actions)

Ex. A colleague suggests a policy that feels punitive in nature, and it does not align with the institutional vision.

1 **Listen to your body and yourself.** We need to assess our emotions and beliefs to understand what compels us to speak truth. For instance, why do you feel compelled to offer another perspective or add your contributions to the conversation? Who does your perspective benefit? Are you equipped with research, adequate information, or lived experiences to navigate this conversation? Are you emotionally ready for the dialogue or potential responses?
2 **Acknowledge when views, actions, or decisions are misaligned from a school district's vision.** Refer people or teams back to the language of the vision and mission. Discuss the parts of the vision that are misaligned with the decisions that are being made.
3 **Lead with curiosity** utilizing the sentence starters from Chapter 5 (Figure 5.7). Raise critical questions. *How does this decision help us to achieve our vision?*
4 **Determine the productivity level of the conversation, assessing if more dialogue is needed.** If an issue is being introduced for the first time, it may be productive to continue a discussion at a different time and place. I have been in situations where I have addressed things publicly and circled back with individuals to have a deeper conversation in another setting. Sometimes, we must keep chipping away at the conversation and recognize that perspectives do not change overnight (Ex. *I'm glad we were able to put our thoughts on the table. Since we do not have a lot of time left in our meeting, I'm willing to set aside some time to continue the conversation later.*)

Some of us have been with teams long enough to know the hot button issues that will lead to difficult conversations. If I am aware of agenda items in advance and can predict the reactions within the room, it does not hurt to process talking points with a trusted colleague prior to a meeting. When you know a particular subject matter will ramp up emotions, it can be helpful to have allyship and support if you decide to speak truth. For example, school discipline was a topic that would usually bring out a variance of perspectives. There were colleagues who leaned toward zero-tolerance policies and others who promoted proactive discipline approaches or restorative practices.

Prior to leadership meetings that focused on school discipline, one of my colleagues and I would connect and strategize as a result of our shared beliefs about social-emotional learning (SEL) and proactive measures. We could count on colleagues challenging our perspectives through questions that involved our own children: *Would you want a student who is throwing chairs to remain in a classroom with your child?* Therefore, we often talked prior to meetings and openly discussed how our responses should connect to the conditions needed for learning. (Ex. *Of course, no one wants their child to be harmed in a classroom and safety is a priority. And, we still need to understand the conditions leading to these outbursts and what we can put in place to ensure that all students experience success. Suspensions provide temporary relief, but what changes when the student returns? What can we do within our systems to change behavioral outcomes? What else can be done?*) Sometimes it is helpful to have a colleague affirm and echo your thoughts in critical conversations.

Navigating Community Pushback

> **Scenario:** *DEI work is relatively new to a school community (e.g., new DEI position or committees are developed) and exists in an area where oppositional groups or community members are strategically working together to weaponize efforts.*

Some of us live in communities where residents have organized and created well-funded parental rights groups to advocate against DEI initiatives. I lived in a county where multiple parent groups established a strong social media presence to promote propaganda and 'expose' inclusionary work within school districts. This was the same county where the organization, Moms for Liberty, made national headlines for quoting Adolf Hitler in their newsletter (Adair, 2023). These oppositional groups will take a beautiful classroom lesson with themes of diversity appreciation (*teaching point= show human dignity to all people*) and market it as a form of indoctrination (*show human dignity to all people= schools are teaching your kids to change their sex, and hate their country*). At some point, we have to reclaim our power and not allow others to rewrite the story of what we are doing to support the growth and well-being of children. If you are working in a similar community where vocal minorities exist to hinder efforts, consider the following steps to create the culture of 'transparency' that oppositional groups are advocating for:

1 **Determine as a district equity team how you will share your story, including phases of implementation, protocols, and timelines for disseminating public information.** The first phase may include collaborative work with a school district's public relations team, developing a storyboard that details the historical background behind the district's DEI initiatives. Many school districts have been immersed in the work of creating inclusive environments long before the language was weaponized. Therefore, it is helpful to discuss the history of your district's DEI work. There are people who will scream over an acronym, but will applaud a school's annual event for Disability Awareness Month, not knowing that is indeed, DEI. When we own our narrative and take a strategic approach to storytelling, we can combat misinformation by overwhelming people with truth.

   The storyboard should address the following questions:
   - What inspired inclusionary work within the district?
   - Why are diversity, equity, and inclusion an integral part of the district's work?
   - Which school district goals align with inclusionary work and why?
   - What progress has been made from DEI efforts?
   - How do all students benefit from efforts to create an inclusive, affirming environment?
   - What does DEI work look like in action within schools?

   If you work in an institution that no longer uses equity literacy, consider the following questions for your storyboard. The objective is to articulate the vision, goals, and assets of a school district in relation to diversity, equity, and inclusion.
   - Why is it important for students to feel connected to their school and have a sense of belonging?
   - Why are partnerships between students, families, teachers, administrators, and community stakeholders critical to the advancement of achievement and student well-being?
   - Which school district goals highlight the importance of creating positive student experiences or outcomes? How will the district achieve those goals?
   - How is the school district working to create access to resources and opportunities for students?

2 **Devise outlets for storytelling and structures to make commitments visible for public consumption.** The second phase involves strategic measures that outline how an organization will tell its story. Storytelling could be in the form of publications, statements, personal narratives, social media, radio or podcast interviews, videos, and public presentations. The following recommendations illustrate how DEI professionals can support the work of shaping narratives and educating communities:
   - **Statements:** Work with school leadership teams and stakeholders to develop a joint statement with school board members that reiterates the district's mission to create an inclusive environment with the intent of dispelling misinformation. For example, when the anti-CRT movement surfaced, I worked in a district where a joint statement was made between our leadership team, community coalition, and school board to combat misinformation. An effective strategy is an arranged meeting with your superintendent to define an issue and evaluate the potential benefits of issuing a statement.
   - **Timeline graphic:** Develop an interactive timeline graphic of DEI work that could be displayed on a district's website. This could include historic information about the school district (e.g., year it was founded, demographics, year of desegregation, etc.), DEI initiatives, partnerships, and the development and purpose of equity teams. The graphic could demonstrate the multifaceted approaches to inclusionary work and how efforts have evolved over time, *even in our current political context.* This strategy also conveys the argument that DEI has been a historic endeavor.
   - **Publications:** Develop publications or include information in a district newsletter that demonstrates DEI in action as related to district goals. Name the aspects of DEI that are visible and prioritized within schools. Ex. *We are committed to creating an inclusive environment where students and families have a sense of belonging. Our commitment is demonstrated through ongoing focus groups where leaders are actively learning from families, etc.* Note that the acronym is not listed in the example, yet DEI is implied in that statement. There are ways to work around oppressive systems.
   - **School board meetings:** Highlight the happenings or achievements of students, staff, or families during school board meetings and how those experiences relate to district goals supporting DEI work.

- **Social media:** Promote DEI initiatives intentionally through social media, helping community members to have a visualization of efforts in action.
- **Promotional videos:** Create a video series where parents, students, and staff share personal accounts about why they chose their district and how schools are working toward goals and equitable practices.
- **Spotlight groups who are working to advance equity:** Highlight the work of equity-based teams, coaches, or parental organizations that support the mission of just educational outcomes.
- **Publicity:** Interview with journalists (who are credible and have a record of uplifting school districts) to highlight the work happening within the district and how DEI initiatives benefit all students.
- **Cultural and religious observances:** Acknowledge cultural and religious observances via social media posts or district newsletters that include corresponding educational resources for families (e.g., community events or book lists that deepen knowledge of cultural observances, etc.)
- **Community-based learning:** Create educational opportunities for families to learn about educational goals, belonging in schools, and other concepts relevant to the district's strategic plan.

3 **Create a plan for the distribution of information.** The third phase involves the timeline for distributing information. School districts in general send a ton of information and updates each week. As a parent, it is sometimes hard to keep up with everything between school and district notifications. A PR team can work on a timeline for distribution. If most district communications and school information are sent on a Friday or Monday, leaders can strategically share equity-related updates on a day where notifications won't get buried by other announcements. In district or school communications/newsletters, there could also be a section that reiterates what was previously shared with the purpose of over-communicating.

When distributing critical information, protocols should be established. For example, before publishing a post on a school-managed social media account, it can be helpful to have someone from an equity team review it. This could ensure that an equity lens was used to review the depictions or messaging of posts prior to publishing. For example, in my professional experience, an educator posted a picture of an educational event that involved children's exploration of police vehicles. The educator, who identified as white, was seated in the front of the vehicle with another white student, while the Black students were in the rear seats of the police car. While the photo was not taken with malicious intent nor posted on the school's social media account, its portrayal carried unintended negative implications that caught the attention of parents and district leaders. Sometimes it can be helpful to have a vetting process for publications. We can recognize students without compromising their privacy or sending negative signals.

People in Positions of Power Are Not Invested in Your Work

Scenario: *DEI practitioner works within a district that promotes a mission of building inclusive and responsive environments, yet discovers that executive leadership and board members are misaligned with the mission and are actively working to sabotage efforts.*

It is not uncommon to be hired into a school district with leaders who 'talk the talk,' but rarely 'walk the walk.' Some of us may be in environments where people showcase equity buzzwords in statements, but it is not a common language within organizational culture. Unfortunately, some of us may also work in districts where school board members or other educational leaders deliberately obstruct our efforts to be inclusive. In these scenarios, shifts may only happen with external pressure from community stakeholders. The same external pressure that is used to eliminate books within school libraries or curriculum could be utilized for actions on the right side of history. We can empower community stakeholders to become civically engaged and nurture their advocacy. When a community mobilizes and demands accountability, change is possible.

The following steps are a significant risk. I want to reiterate that I do not want to be the source of anyone losing financial security, health insurance, or their dream job. However, if your risk assessment index rate is low and you believe external pressure could move the needle, you may want to engage in community mobilization tactics. It is also important for you to know that my recommendations are based on my experiences. I would not tell you to try something I have not done.

1. **Organize community-focus groups.** Facilitate an environment where families can share school experiences and work collaboratively to discuss strategies for improved educational systems. Discuss district updates and efforts that are being made (if any) to address emerging concerns.

2 **Empower families to build a network.** There is power in community. Create a document or form for families to opt into a collective that receives district updates and issues that require advocacy. School families can provide their names and contact information.
3 **Designate one or two parents or caregivers to serve as community liaisons, who will work closely with you (DEI practitioner) and families who opted into the advocacy group.** The liaisons are positioned as community leaders who develop mechanisms (e.g., private/public social media pages, email distribution lists, etc.) to keep members of the collective abreast of district happenings, policy development, or updates in state legislative sessions. Liaisons will not only keep community members informed but will also provide action steps that outline how families can get involved in advocacy.
4 **Develop a trusting relationship with the liaisons.** The act of building trust requires us to have good judgment and wisdom in our interactions and communications with others. In a trusting relationship, we (DEI practitioners) can be transparent about the obstacles we are facing and offer liaisons pathways for advocacy. Liaisons should feel encouraged to mobilize others. This could include the work of inviting families to write letters to executive leaders or to speak at board meetings. No matter the strategies, liaisons can inspire community stakeholders to apply pressure toward change.
5 **Remain objective in your approach with liaisons.** Ensure that communications align with the mission of supporting all children and leave out personal opinions. Even in a trusting professional relationship, one should still consider their positionality and filter within communications.

This is an approach that I used personally in my first role after learning that allyship and solidarity did not exist among district leaders and school board members. School board members were actively sabotaging my efforts, flooding my mailbox with propaganda, and encouraging the community to actively petition against my role. Since internal organizational support was lacking and no one had the courage to challenge board members or the vocal minority, I had to find a way to protect myself and the impactful work I was doing, as measured by students. There were strategies that I needed to implement to sustain progress, and I had to develop a shield to get those objectives done. Therefore, I decided to build a community of people around me and empowered others to work alongside me while I still had the stamina to fight.

It is important to note that I also have a history of reading people and their dispositions well. Personally, I believe that wisdom comes from my grandmother, who could accurately unpack a person's disposition in a matter of minutes. I am rarely surprised by people's actions or behaviors. Therefore, after meeting many families through events and focus groups, it was fairly easy to find individuals who could serve as co-conspirators and walk in lockstep with my advocacy. If you have a hard time reading individuals and struggle to build trust, this may not be the best approach for you. I do not want you to find out that your so-called co-conspirators are actually opps who are leveraging your words to develop a movement against you.

The liaisons who worked closely with me would fiercely advocate for change. If board members petitioned against my work, they would develop their own petitions and acquire signatures to sustain my efforts. They mobilized to get others involved in board meetings and became active during board elections to campaign for equity-minded leaders. I did not feel one ounce of guilt telling people—*who I trusted*—what I needed to support children. In fact, I endured more than I should have and extended my time within that particular district because of their advocacy and steadfast support.

Scenario: *DEI practitioner works within a district that promotes a mission of inclusion, yet discovers that executive leadership and board members are actively working to sabotage efforts. External allyship is non-existent. School community members, within and outside of the system, are petitioning against efforts and causing harm that impacts wellness and physical health.*

Some of us may experience isolation within our positions, where we feel as if we are stranded on a deserted island. We are left to defend ourselves with limited resources and lack the power to make changes. Not only does organizational support lack, but we may also work in an area where people are actively pursuing our downfall. If you work in this type of environment and lack community support, you may need to consider initiating a critical conversation or new job opportunities. Regardless of the path you choose, safeguarding your mental health and asserting your voice or choices are essential steps toward reclaiming your power. We must also recognize that some endings are necessary for our growth and wholeness.

Within my ancestral playbook, I note the quote that many attribute to Zora Neale Hurston: *If you are silent about your pain, they'll kill you and say you enjoyed it.* We cannot allow people to harm or disparage us and rewrite our stories through their lens. When it's time to make an exit, think carefully about how you'll take control of your narrative. It is important to think about your peace of mind and professional reputation. You may want to own your truth through a blog or take a risk (because we know that anyone can weaponize our stories or use it against us) and share your story with someone who will publish it. There is power in sharing our stories. We do not have to allow another person's words to dictate who we are. If you feel inclined to resign from a position and do not want others to create a narrative about your experiences, consider how you will share your own story.

Dena Simmons, the founder of LiberatED, was a part of a group (shout out to Lisa Harton and Dennisha Murff) that co-presented with me at the National Council of Teachers of English (NCTE) conference in Boston (2024). We facilitated a session called, *Saving Ourselves: How Black Women Educators Change and Heal from Unjust Systems.* During the session, Simmons specifically talked about the importance of owning our stories. She shared her experiences from working in Yale University and the racism she encountered leading up to her resignation. Furthermore, she discussed how she decided to share her narrative, encouraging the audience to be critical of who receives our stories. Not every journalist or news outlet has the best intentions, and we need to evaluate who can receive access to our experiences. Here some considerations for walking in our truth following the departure from an organization.

1 **Determine how you will tell your story.** When we acknowledge our stories and process our emotions, we allow room for peace and healing to enter our lives. Inner peace starts with us reclaiming our power and regaining agency.
2 **Consider who should have access to your story.** We do not owe anyone our story, so it is important to consider our audience and the outlets for sharing our story. When I resigned from both of my DEI roles under different circumstances, reporters reached out to inquire more information. I denied them access to my story, considering my evaluation of their publications. We exist in times where people may weaponize our words for their own agenda or clickbait. Therefore, choose your outlets wisely.
3 **Remember, our truth can be a light for others.** When we share our stories within a community, we begin to recognize that we are not alone. During the same NCTE conference, I talked about my first DEI role and how I decided to save myself. Following the conference, I made connections with several individuals who discussed their experiences with similar challenges. They were grateful to know their experiences were not in isolation and found community in others. Our stories foster human connections and solidarity.

Storytelling provides a sense of connection and empowerment. I remember learning about Sarah Inama's story, a teacher from West Ada Middle School, who was asked to remove inclusive posters by school administrators. Inama eventually resigned to walk in her values, noting that *it is extremely disturbing and embarrassing to see a district prioritize appeasing individuals with racist perspectives over celebrating the diversity and beauty of all our students* (Flandro, 2025, para 3). Her words were inspiring to me and provided hope. Despite rising policies that are designed to diminish DEI work, we do not have to be complicit and bend to the will of people who promote dehumanization. Inama's story shows us that we can stay true to our beliefs and shape our own future. Our story does not end after leaving an institution that is misaligned with our values. Rather, we start a new chapter with a renewed sense of self and purpose. We all benefit from stories that empower us to walk in our truth.

Reshaping DEI Work

Another method for combating resistance is the reshaping of DEI initiatives, roles, departments, and goals with executive leadership and school board approval. If an acronym is the source of controversy and causes the withholding of funds from government entities, then a reasonable option may be to shift the language. As discussed in Chapter 2, there are many organizations that focus on inclusive and equitable practices with departments or committees that have historically not been labeled as DEI. If a name change positions your organization to maintain its commitments and funding, then it may be helpful to rename departments or roles. This strategy reduces the negative political connotations and helps school districts to remain in compliance with legal requirements.

The reorganization of departments or responsibilities may be another option. Many DEI administrators are responsible for overseeing civil rights, such as Title IX, VI, etc. If human resources (HR) absorbed those duties, DEI practitioners could concentrate their efforts on instructional systems and leadership development. The shift from Title IX and VI responsibilities could dissociate the DEI practitioner from the notion that their work solely revolves around claims of racial and gender discrimination. DEI practitioners should be active in other departments, particularly teaching and learning, to ensure an equity lens in pedagogical approaches. Some of my colleagues have also experienced title changes, and their responsibilities have shifted to align with the language of their renamed positions. While their duties remain largely the same, they are embedded in different initiatives and projects.

Reshaping DEI work could also mean reframing language within policy goals. Despite glaring racial disparities in schools, we exist in a time where the Office for Civil Rights has been weaponized to denote racial justice efforts as discriminatory. In efforts to comply with federal guidelines, racial equity concepts may have to be embedded into strategies and discussed in staff meetings rather than being written as standalone goals. Under the umbrella of belonging, conversations about racial equity and educational justice can still emerge. Students and staff cannot have a sense of belonging if they are actively experiencing racism and other forms of dehumanization. Professional learning communities (PLCS) should still be a place where we objectively discuss data, including racial disparities.

As I share thoughts about reshaping DEI, I must be honest in naming it as my least favorite approach. It feels like a gut punch to be forced to follow guidelines from people who uphold racist and other problematic ideologies. However, through consulting relationships and working with schools, I do understand the fears and know that many government officials have used artificial intelligence to comb through school websites to ensure the elimination of equity literacy (often threatening schools when threads of DEI are visible). Some of my colleagues have even been told to remove DEI terminology found on district publications in order to maintain funding for vital student programs. Although districts can pushback (based on Jessica Heiser's interview in Chapter 6), I understand the hesitations. Between ongoing threats and community pressure, DEI practitioners and educational leaders are in a tight spot.

I also struggle with the notion that school districts can only commit to actions that satisfy conservative or right-wing groups. The disregard for our professionalism, judgment, and areas of expertise is unsettling. No one wants to work in an environment where their actions are directed by individuals who have no background in their field—and we currently have many people outside of education calling the shots and telling educators how to teach! What happens when oppositional groups attack our attempts to reshape DEI language, roles, and responsibilities? Do we constantly change our course and stance to appease people who lack a moral compass and refuse to see the humanity of others?

When you are committed to telling truth, it is hard to accept any approach that does not feel authentic. Many of us believe that if we cannot name disparities, then it is hard to address inequities and hold people accountable. It is even more devastating to see the elimination of programs, affinity spaces, and the banning of books, knowing those decisions excluded the voices of those impacted. However, as I wrestle with all these thoughts, I am reminded of my ancestral playbook. I recognize that grassroots movements positioned many activists to work behind the scenes rather than in the spotlight. Additionally, activists of liberatory movements did not need to label their efforts with an acronym to make an impact. Therefore, no matter the barrier, we can find a way to press forward, build community, and show up for the people we serve. We can still rise and make progress against all odds.

Protecting Our Peace: You Won't Break My Soul

Mental clarity is critical while navigating resistance. It is no secret that operating in a state of constant stress is not good for our well-being or health. Protecting our peace involves the creation of support systems, boundaries, and intentional activities to manage stress. We must be unapologetic in taking care of ourselves and stay connected to what truly matters—*family, friends, mental health, physical health, etc.* It is important to renew our pursuit for wholeness and nurture our inner peace.

I learned this lesson the hard way during my first role as a Chief Equity and Inclusion Officer. When I went home, I often felt the weariness and heaviness from my job. One support system that helped was affinity meetings with other DEI practitioners. I appreciated being in a space where I could unwind with other individuals who understood my challenges in school. In my career, I met with two different groups that served as a source of healing for me. My family is also a refuge and a strong source of joy in my life. Our weekend adventures, movie nights, and walks around the neighborhood have been a remedy in lowering high levels of cortisol. I am not as consistent as I would like to be with my workouts, but exercising is another great way to relieve stress. No matter the challenges we face, we cannot lose ourselves as a result of a job or toxic individuals.

The following accounts are provided by practitioners who describe their approaches to self-care in an anti-DEI climate. We must remember to rest and let things go that are not within our control. I used to hold on to everything (and my husband will say that I still fall into that trap at times), but I am working hard to release stressors in effort to improve my health. As a parent, there is nothing I want more than to see my child grow up and become a well-rounded adult. Therefore, I know my life needs more balance, mindfulness, and activities that prioritize wellness.

Here are other things DEI practitioners are doing to protect their peace:

> *As a DEI practitioner, protecting my peace has been essential in sustaining both my well-being and effectiveness in this work. One of the most impactful strategies I've embraced is setting clear boundaries—around my time, energy, and emotional availability. This includes defining what's in my control, saying no when necessary, and ensuring I carve out space for rest and joy outside of work. Self-care practices like journaling, mindfulness, physical activity, and unplugging from the constant stream of information help me stay grounded. Equally important is leaning on my circle of family and close friends. Their support reminds me of who I am beyond the role and helps me stay connected to love, laughter, and perspective. When facing anti-DEI*

rhetoric or pushback, I intentionally return to these relationships to refill my cup and protect my mental and emotional space. I also find strength in community—connecting with fellow DEI practitioners for encouragement, perspective, and strategy sharing. Regular reflection and, at times, therapy, have helped me process tough moments and stay centered in my purpose. All of this combined allows me to keep showing up with intention, clarity, and heart.

-Joi Odom, Diversity Equity and Inclusion Director, Washington

My peace comes from meeting on a regular basis with those of like-minds so "they" won't have you thinking you're the one who's crazy.

-Patricia Payne, Director of the IPS Office of Strategic and Educational Excellence, Indiana (formerly a well-known Office of Racial Equity within the community)

Prioritize that work stays at work. Remember that when you experience backlash or harmful commentary, it is not a reflection of you or who you are - maintaining positive and affirming definitions of self are necessary. Rely on the people you trust and keep the circle small. Build and sustain affinity spaces for recharge and community. Build mental health and vacation days into your calendar far in advance. If something comes up, move the date, but don't delete it.

-Ayva Thomas, Executive Director of Organizational Change and Student Advancement and Ranna Harb, Organizational Change and Student Advancement Specialist, Washington

Karate, gun range, read, walk, pray and research to validate my efforts. Family & church. And THERAPY. Commune with like-minded war-torn equity leaders.

-John Marshall, Chief Equity Officer, Kentucky

Sometimes You Have to Save Yourself

Through monthly affinity group meetings, I was able to connect with multiple Black women leaders in administrative DEI roles in education who shared similar experiences. Most encountered ongoing resistance in the workplace and lacked support from supervisors. Within this particular working group, all of us talked about the challenges of pushing for change as Black women leaders in predominantly white organizations. We discussed the emotional toll advocacy took on our bodies.

Months into the development of our affinity group, we learned that one of our colleagues was found dead in her home. She died of heart failure, which was distressing to our group, considering her remarks about workplace stress. Through conversations beyond affinity spaces, I have been exposed to more stories of DEI practitioners living with health complications. While I am unable to establish a direct correlation between advocacy work and health outcomes or speculate the underlying cause of specific health conditions, it is well-documented that stress can cause high blood pressure, illness, and harm our physical well-being.

Sometimes we must save ourselves in the face of resistance. We have to give ourselves the gift of stillness and rest. This could mean taking time away from work to restore our bodies and minds. Saving ourselves could also entail advocacy to reorganize our responsibilities in a way that provides more balance. We should focus on conditions that support our well-being. Personally, I struggled to preserve my well-being in my first DEI role. I was not mentally well while encountering complaints, petitions against my work, and online harassment. Whenever I entered the parking lot at my workplace, I felt physically ill and anticipated the worst. For me, the prioritization of wellness looked like closing one chapter via a resignation and starting a new role within a different district.

Saving ourselves involves radical self-love. We love ourselves enough to choose freedom over conformity. I often think about the song, Defying Gravity from the musical, Wicked. The lyrics, *And if I'm flying solo, at least I'm flying free,* make me emotional and capture how I have moved in this world. It has not been easy to 'fly solo' and walk away from institutions. To be completely vulnerable, there were times when I was mad at myself for not being complicit. When you see people selling their souls and advancing while you remain true to yourself and struggle, you do have moments of self-doubt and question your decisions. Now, I recognize that walking in my values is the best gift I can give to myself. It has opened doors for different opportunities, partnerships, and authentic connections.

Do not fall for the trap and believe that you must accept mistreatment or dehumanizing conditions to move forward within your career. We owe ourselves the opportunity to develop or work in school environments that are inclusive and honor the full humanity of others. We deserve to work in school districts where people want to create lasting change and model culturally responsive behaviors. We all deserve school districts that are invested in the protection of children's rights. We deserve to work in spaces where we can make a difference.

In the spirit of saving ourselves and protecting our peace, reflect on the words of Joi Odom, a Director of Diversity, Equity, and Inclusion in

Washington. Although our work is challenging, you are never alone. Find your people, seek joy, and be authentically you.

> *To DEI practitioners navigating unjust systems in an anti-DEI climate: protect your spirit. This work is not for the faint of heart. You're often asked to fix systems you didn't break, to educate people who resist learning, and to advocate for change in spaces that weren't designed for inclusion. You will be challenged, questioned, dismissed, and sometimes even targeted—for simply telling the truth.*
>
> *But here's what I know: you're not crazy, and you're not alone. The gaslighting is real. The pushback is real. The exhaustion is real. But so is the impact of your presence. Just by showing up and refusing to shrink, you're making space for others to breathe, to belong, to be seen. So here's my advice:*
>
> *Be unapologetically rooted in your values. Name what's happening, even when it makes people uncomfortable. Document everything. Find your people—those who affirm your work and your humanity. Set boundaries fiercely. Rest deeply. And never let anyone convince you that this work isn't necessary or that you're asking for too much. You are asking for dignity. For justice. For the bare minimum. And that is not too much.*
>
> *Lead with love, but don't confuse love with silence. Sometimes love looks like naming harm. Sometimes love is walking away when the system refuses to shift. And always—love yourself enough not to carry more than your share of the burden.*
>
> *We are planting seeds—even when it feels like we're shouting into the wind. And those seeds matter. They grow in ways we may never see, but they grow. Speak truth. Stand tall. Keep going. You're building something bigger than the moment you're in.*

With Gratitude

If you are actively working in a DEI role, please know that I am grateful for you and your leadership. Thank you for being a light during dark times in our political climate.

Oftentimes, DEI work is a thankless job. It is my hope that you have felt seen throughout many chapters of this book and recognize your value in this movement for justice.

You deserve an environment that recognizes your gifts, worth, and humanity. You also deserve peace and restoration following days that challenge your wellness or spirit. My hope is that you listen to your body and find refuge through community. You matter, and your brilliance is needed to impact the field of education and the lives of children. Thank you for speaking truth to power and for being a part of a movement that chooses courage and centers humanity. You are exactly who we need in this moment of history.

Chapter Highlights

1. As practitioners working in unjust systems, *we must know when to push, when to pause, and when to protect our peace*. There are times when we need to advocate for change and moments when we need to pause to recollect our thoughts or gain different perspectives. Do not feel obligated to react to everything. Consider areas where you should invest your energy, and know when you need to walk away to protect your peace.
2. Mental preparation is key to dealing with adversity. It is important for us to know ourselves and our emotional response to conflict. Being mentally prepared also involves introspective work where we reflect on our leadership and how it was shaped. We should also consider the wisdom we have acquired from elders, ancestors, and mentors, and think about the legacy we want to leave behind.
3. We can combat resistance with truth. Data offers clarity and factual information, while storytelling appeals to the heart. We need to eliminate the misinformation that hinders the advancement of equity.
4. Political climates force us to think about the reshaping of DEI work. No matter what is needed to abide by laws, be true to the mission of supporting all students and their identities. Be clear in explaining shifts and changes to staff as well, so they are not under the impression that DEI work no longer lives within their school or district.
5. Do not feel ashamed to walk away from a role or responsibilities to protect your peace and well-being. People are counting on you to be here for the long haul. Radical self-love means giving yourself the permission to let certain people, places, or things go. There is work needed everywhere, and you can find a district that values what you bring to the table.

Mirror Work

1. Review questions from the Figure 7.1. Consider what you have learned about yourself, including areas of growth. What boundaries will you establish for yourself in efforts to maintain stamina in your advocacy?
2. Consider ancestors who are a guiding light for your work. What legacy do you want to leave behind as you work toward building just schools?

References

Adair, K. (2023, June 22) Indiana chapter of Moms of Liberty features Hitler quote in first newsletter. https://www.wfyi.org/news/articles/indiana-chapter-of-moms-for-liberty-features-hitler-quote-in-first-newsletter

Allen, G. (2022, February 1). *Remembering a forgotten fighter for civil rights: Harry t. Moore*. National Public Radio. https://www.npr.org/2022/02/01/1077198365/remembering-a-forgotten-fighter-for-civil-rights-harry-t-moore

Buchanan-Rivera, E. (2022). *Identity affirming classrooms: Spaces that center humanity*. Routledge Publishing.

Buchanan-Rivera, E., Harton, L., Murff, D., & Simmons, D. (2024, November 21). *Saving Ourselves: How Black Women Educators Change and Heal from Unjust Systems*. [Conference Session]. National Council of English Teachers, Boston, MA.

Charron, K. (2012). *Freedom's teacher: The life of Septima Clark*. The University of North Carolina Press.

Collins, M., & Tamarkin, C. (1990). *The Marva Collins' Way: Returning to excellence in education*. Jeremy P. Tarcher, Inc.

Flandro, C. (2025, July 18). Inama, teacher at heart of poster controversy, resigns. *Idaho Education News*, www.idahoednews.org/west-idaho/inama-teacher-at-heart-of-poster-controversy-resigns/.

Gandini, L., et al. (2015). *In the spirit of the studio: Learning from the Atelier of Reggio Emilia*. Teachers College.

hooks, b. (2001). *All about love*. Harper Collins Publishing.

Kelley, R. (2022). *Freedom dreams: The Black radical imagination*. Beacon Press.

Lorde, A. (1984). *The transformation of silence into language and action*. In *Sister outsider: Essays and speeches* (pp. 40–44). Crossing Press. (Original work published 1978)

Malaguzzi, L. (1998). History, ideas, and basic philosophy: An interview with Lella Gandini. (pp. 49–97). In Edwards, C., Gandini, L. & Forman, G. (Ed.). *The hundred languages of children: The Reggio approach – Advanced reflections* (2nd ed.). Ablex Publishing.

New Mexico Historic Women Marker Program. (2026). *Mela Lucero Leger*. https://www.nmhistoricwomen.org/new-mexico-historic-women/mela-lucero-leger/

Theoarris, J. (2018). *A beautiful and terrible history: The uses and misuses of civil rights history*. Beacon Press.

Thorpe, C. (2022, March). Leading While Black. https://www.nassp.org/publication/principal-leadership/volume-22-2021-2022/principal-leadership-march-2022/leading-while-black/

Wilkerson, I. (2020). *The warmth of other Suns: The epic story of America's great migration*. Penguin Books.

Epilogue

A Letter to K-12 Superintendents

Dear Superintendent,

There are many benefits to hiring someone who can streamline efforts to promote diversity, equity, and inclusion. When a practitioner has experience with organizational change and carries a lens for justice, educational equity has the potential to shift from a symbolic gesture to sustainable, impactful practices that drive achievement and enriching experiences for students. It is helpful to have a thought partner within a school district who operates with a strategic, collective approach to critically examine and transform educational systems.

Unfortunately, many school districts hire DEI practitioners without knowledge of what those roles need to succeed. One person does not hold the power to change inequitable structures, practices, or policies. School districts must clarify the roles and responsibilities of DEI practitioners, and ensure that all educational staff actively commit to the work of improving systems and pedagogical approaches. Every member within a school district should feel compelled to remove institutional barriers that harm the outcomes of students. Importantly, if school districts want to retain and attract justice-minded practitioners, educational leaders must create conditions that make DEI work credible and sustainable.

DEI practitioners cannot operate effectively within an environment if they do not receive support from their superintendents. It is important for superintendents to demonstrate how they value equity work, conveying why DEI practitioner roles are needed and how positions will be leveraged within the school district to support educational goals. DEI practitioners also deserve access to spaces where decisions are made, including participation within senior leadership teams. The work of creating just systems cannot be delegated or viewed as a checklist, and should live in the office of the superintendent. Therefore, when opposition or forms of resistance emerge, there's a leadership structure in place where problems are absorbed and addressed by all members. Demonstrating visible support and ownership of a DEI practitioner's work reinforces that the promotion of diversity, equity, and inclusion is a collective approach rather than the responsibility of one individual.

DEI practitioners require leadership teams where people walk in values of justice. It is important for practitioners to witness their superintendents leading by example. Superintendents should model advocacy, inclusive practices, and asset-based language, demonstrating how DEI lives in their professionalism and everyday life. The communication, decision-making, and prioritizations of leaders signal the viability of DEI work. Please consider how leadership dispositions and beliefs impact the efforts and well-being of DEI practitioners.

When shared power and leadership are evident, DEI practitioner roles have the potential to foster the collaborative work that is needed to create affirming and responsive environments. Please consider your power and how it is used to make DEI an integral and viable part of educational systems.

Best regards,

Dr. EBR

A former Pre-K-12 Chief Equity and Inclusion Officer

Appendix A

Working Document Example of Equity Literacy

Terminology for a Common Language within Equity Teams
A word bank could be created and housed in a learning management system (LMS) as a working document to help educational staff understand terminology for equity literacy. As a pro-tip, DEI practitioners could also link articles, videos, and graphics under terms within online platforms to enhance understandings. The following terms are words I defined for faculty and staff in educational contexts. This is not a full list, but merely a sample. As questions emerged about equity literacy, I would add new terms to the word bank.
Bigotry: *intolerance toward those who hold different opinions or an unreasonable attachment to a belief* ***Discrimination:*** *unfavorable or unfair treatment toward an individual or group based on their race, ethnicity, national origin, religion, socioeconomic status, language, age, gender, physical or mental abilities, sexual orientation, or other statuses* ***Diversity****: a numerical representation of differences* ***Educational Equity:*** *focuses on the removal of barriers, ensuring equal access, sharing power, and affirming identities to support student success* ***Inclusion:*** *the act of being included within a group or structure* ***Institutionalized Racism:*** *refers to the way educational, economic, legal, and political institutions systemically benefit some racial groups while disadvantaging others, producing racially inequitable outcomes* ***Prejudice:*** *a prejudgment toward individuals or groups based on limited knowledge and experience* ***Privilege:*** *unearned power and advantages granted to a particular group based on their identity or status* ***Race:*** *a social construct that divides people into distinct groups based on physical characteristics* ***Sexism:*** *prejudice, stereotyping, or discrimination on the basis of sex* ***Stereotype:*** *a positive or negative set of beliefs held by an individual about the characteristics of a certain group* ***Title IX:*** *prohibits discrimination based on sex in education programs and activities that receive federal financial assistance*

Appendix B

Application for School-Based Equity Teams

Application Questions for School-Based Equity Teams
Here are questions to consider for an application-based process to assemble equity teams in schools. ***Note***: The questions could be structured in an electronic form that is reviewed by administrative teams. As stated in Chapter 4, an application process is not my preferred method. However, it can help to generate a cadre of highly-motivated leaders who have the will and skills to build coalitions that move the needle toward equity.
1. Describe your interest in joining a school-based equity team. 2. What does educational justice mean to you? What does it look like in action? 3. Describe leadership experiences in addressing inequities in schools. 4. Review our school's improvement plan. What is one area of focus that needs a revision in strategy development? Why? 5. How do you actively promote diversity, equity, or inclusion in your everyday life?

Appendix C

Beginning and End-of-Year Assessment for School-Based Equity Teams

School-based equity teams could use this rubric to assess their collective efforts, areas of focus, and school culture. The outcomes should serve as a catalyst for discussions pertaining to strategies and opportunities for growth within staff meetings and professional learning communities. This tool should be implemented at the beginning and end of the year as a progress monitoring tool toward school/district goals.

	Developing	Progressing	Advanced
Physical Environment	The physical environment may not adequately support conditions (e.g., psychological, instructional, social, etc.) for student learning.	Diversity is recognized and celebrated within the school environment through various cultural, religious, and familial contexts. Teachers intentionally think about the design of space and create conditions for learning.	The physical environment reflects students' capabilities, identities, and lived experiences. Educators make their beliefs about diversity, equity, and inclusion visible within the classroom as noted by the layout and design of space. Students co-construct their learning environments with teachers and school leaders.

Data-Driven Practices	Data is used within professional learning communities (PLC), school improvement teams (SIP), equity teams, and grade-level/ department meetings. However, there remains an absence of thoroughly developed discourse that yields to actionable strategies and productive outcomes.	Data is used within professional learning communities (PLC), school improvement teams (SIP), equity teams, and grade-level/department meetings where action steps and progress monitoring tools are determined. Although inequities are identified and discussed, these conversations may require more depth and preparation (e.g., teachers and staff feel equipped to discuss disparities).	Data informs essential discussions about instructional methodologies and systemic inequities. Educators and staff conduct thorough analyses of systems and are prepared to address disparities in impactful ways. Diverse data sets—disaggregated by factors such as race, ability, and language—are evaluated to design targeted interventions, addressing both the social and academic needs of students. Enrollment, discipline, and programmatic data are also reviewed to initiate conversations about inclusive practices.
Pedagogical Practices and Curriculum	Instructional lessons may lack differentiation and cultural responsivity. Singular stories are evident in curricular materials, prompting teachers to use supplemental resources that are not vetted.	The curriculum incorporates a wide range of perspectives, and teachers intentionally connect learning to students' lived experiences. Teachers tailor instruction to meet students' needs, yet may require additional support to effectively facilitate conversations about historical, political, and social issues.	Teachers engage in mirror work and consider their biases while implementing instruction. Multiple perspectives are included within the curriculum and teachers feel equipped to navigate conversations about humanity, history, and current events. Students are invited to process the world around them and make visual representations of their learning. Differentiation is evident and visible in student outcomes.

(*Continued*)

	Developing	Progressing	Advanced
Student Relationships	Teachers and staff operate under the assumption that students inherently understand how to behave, respond, or engage with others. There is an emphasis on maintaining order rather than human development, building connections, and modeling expectations.	While teachers and staff acknowledge and value students' identities, histories, and lived experiences, they may find it challenging to confront institutional barriers that contribute to marginalization. Even though community-building is prioritized, the harm some students encounter may go unaddressed.	Students maintain trusting relationships with teachers and staff, and report a sense of psychological safety as indicated by climate surveys, student interviews, or focus groups. Student voice is integral to school-based decision-making and improvement initiatives. Additionally, students receive instruction in leadership and advocacy skills to help foster an inclusive community.
Community Engagement	School personnel organize numerous community-based events. While these initiatives are positive and aligned with institutional objectives, they may not fully account for the barriers families encounter within school systems, nor are they always developed with accessibility considerations as a priority.	Families are invited and encouraged to actively participate in the educational experiences of their child or children. School publications and events are culturally responsive and accessible to all families.	Families and community partners are encouraged to participate in collective work that is designed to improve educational systems. Their input shapes a more inclusive school community and equitable outcomes. Parental and caregiver involvement extends beyond attending events; it includes having meaningful opportunities to contribute to student success.

Equity-focused Leadership	School leaders endorse initiatives that advance diversity, equity, and inclusion; however, competing demands and responsibilities often limit their visibility and direct involvement in these efforts. As a result, staff may be uncertain about their leaders' perspectives, as these beliefs are not clearly communicated.	School leaders regularly attend meetings pertaining to student achievement and support diversity, equity, and inclusion initiatives. However, it is challenging to hold others accountable and critical conversations with staff lack. Staff committed to equitable practices may feel frustrated while doing intentional work and witnessing others do the bare minimum.	School leaders' beliefs about diversity, equity, and inclusion are visible through rhetoric and actions. Everyone is held accountable for goals toward equitable achievement. Leaders help to facilitate an inclusive work culture where all teachers and staff are motivated to eliminate disparities. Humanizing leadership approaches are evident and encourage people to be their authentic selves in the workplace.

Appendix D

Systems Work Framework with Potential Action Steps

	Area of Focus	Description of Area of Focus	Systems Work (potential actions action steps for improving systems)
Individual	**Learning and Development**	fostering professional and personal growth within each working member of an institution	• curating and sharing resources in a learning management system • creating self-assessments or reflection tools to help staff build a critical consciousness • development of a professional learning series (e.g., webinars, guest speakers, videos created by district or school-based equity teams, book studies, etc.) • development of pathways for anti-bias and anti-racist education (ABAR) • creating equity-learning cohorts (an on-boarding initiative for new staff that involves a monthly cohort meeting where staff have a brave space to talk about DEI-related work)
Institutional	**Climate and Hiring**	systems work to improve practices, policies, and outcomes for students	• development and implementation of school/district climate surveys that are incorporated into strategic plans • development of mentorship programs for students and staff • devising methods for the recruitment and retention of equity-minded staff • creating districtwide wellness initiatives
	Accessibility and Equitable Opportunities		• addressing policies that may marginalize educational staff or students (e.g., behavioral, dress codes, ensuring inclusive language in policies, etc.) • developing a system that monitors student enrollment in programs (e.g., IB, AP/Honors, high ability) in efforts to assess and eliminate disparities

Instructional	**Diversity in the Curriculum and Co-Curriculum**	pedagogical approaches, curriculum, and instructional materials used to advance student achievement	• ensuring that multiple cultural perspectives and diverse worldviews are reflected in the curriculum (ex. coaching curriculum teams or providing an evaluative tool for curriculum departments to review and utilize in curriculum adoption processes) • development of equity walk-throughs and classroom audits • ensuring professional development focuses on differentiation and the removal of deficit ideology
Intercultural Engagement	**Community Partnerships and Engagement**	the work of building capacity, a sense of community, and movements of empowerment among stakeholder groups	• ensuring all families have access to important school information • developing community-based education • devising community forums to honor the voices of stakeholders • creating community coalitions • development of a district calendar that marks events across schools that celebrate student learning • development of leadership 'meet and greets' events to connect with stakeholders

Appendix E

Mockup of Equity Coach Role

Equity Coach Position
Equity coaches **(or any other relevant name)** of **(insert school district)** should demonstrate a commitment to all children, families, and the professional growth of all colleagues through the promotion of equity, social justice, anti-bias education, and inclusionary practices. **(Insert district)** coaches accept and respect cultural differences as outlined in the district's anti-discrimination policy **(insert the actual policy number)**. In collaboration with educational leaders, coaches will jointly develop and implement strategies aimed at eliminating disproportionality in data and addressing institutional barriers or systems that contribute to the marginalization students. **(Insert school district)** coaches are expected to foster a positive school climate and culture that creates an identity-affirming environment for all.
Qualifications
1. Demonstrates in-depth knowledge and understanding of anti-bias and anti-racist education. 2. Actively participates in extensive training and equity-related professional development. 3. Member of an active equity team (school or community-based). 4. Demonstrates effective teaching or leadership, resulting in improved outcomes for students.
Expectations and Responsibilities
1. Serves as a bridge between educational institutions and families, advocating for equitable opportunities among all stakeholders. 2. Conducts and attends all regularly scheduled equity team meetings. 3. Responsible for equity assessments and self-evaluation tools. 4. Works with principal(s) and colleagues to develop a positive school climate. 5. Meets with principal and/or instructional coach quarterly or as often as needed to engage in ongoing conversations about the school's progress and efforts to address disproportionality in data. 6. Creates pathways to amplify the voices of students and families. 7. Encourages a community of adult learners and provides professional development opportunities to enhance understandings of educational justice and equity. 8. Supports teachers to ensure lessons convey diverse, multiple perspectives that connect to students' experiences.

Printable versions of Appendix C and Appendix D are available on the book page on Routledge.com so you can print them for your own use.

For Product Safety Concerns and Information please contact our EU representative GPSR@taylorandfrancis.com
Taylor & Francis Verlag GmbH, Kaufingerstraße 24, 80331 München, Germany

www.ingramcontent.com/pod-product-compliance
Lightning Source LLC
LaVergne TN
LVHW061104130926
847902LV00030B/460
* 9 7 8 1 0 3 2 6 0 9 3 8 6 *